BETWEEN the LINES

Developing critical literacy

Gillian Lovell
Assisted by Lyndall Hough

Dedication
To English teachers everywhere.

Gillian Lovell

Heinemann
A division of Reed International Books Australia Pty Ltd
22 Salmon Street, Port Melbourne, Victoria 3207
World Wide Web hi.com.au
Email info@hi.com.au

Offices in Sydney, Brisbane, Adelaide and Perth.
Associated companies, branches and representatives throughout the world.

© Gillian Lovell 1999
First published 1999
2003 2002 2001 2000
10 9 8 7 6 5 4 3

Copying for educational purposes
The Australian *Copyright Act 1968* (the Act) allows a maximum of one chapter or 10% of this book, whichever is the greater, to be copied by any educational institution for its educational purposes provided that that educational institution (or the body that administers it) has given a remuneration notice to Copyright Agency Limited (CAL) under the Act.

For details of the CAL licence for educational institutions contact CAL, Level 19, 157 Liverpool Street, Sydney, NSW, 2000, tel (02) 9394 7600, fax (02) 9394 7601, email info@copyright.com.au.

Copying for other purposes
Except as permitted under the Act, for example any fair dealing for the purposes of study, research, criticism or review, no part of this book may be reproduced, stored in a retrieval system, or transmitted in any form or by any means without prior written permission. All enquiries should be made to the publisher at the address above.

Publisher: Mark Childs
Editor: Susan Lee
Designer: Lisa Mammola
Cover illustration: Ranya Langenfelds
Photograph researcher: Janet Pheasant

Typeset in 12/15 Clearface Gothic by J&M Typesetting
Film supplied by Type Scan, Adelaide
Printed in Singapore by Kin Keong Printing

National Library of Australia
cataloguing-in-publication data:

Lovell, Gillian.
  Between the lines: developing critical literacy.
  ISBN 0 86462 415 8.

  1. Language arts – Social aspects – Australia. 2. Literacy – Social aspects – Australia. 3. Critical pedagagy – Australia. I. Hough, Lydall. II. Title.

Disclaimer
All the Internet addresses (URLs) given in this book were valid at the time of printing. However, due to the dynamic nature of the Internet, some addresses may have changed, or sites may have ceased to exist since publication. While the authors and publisher regret any inconvenience this may cause readers, no responsibility for any such changes can be accepted by either the authors or the publisher.

Acknowledgments
The author would like to thank Lyndall Hough for her patient reading and critiquing of the manuscript. Her comments were always valuable, often very funny and made revisions much less onerous. The author would also like to thank Mark Childs for his enthusiasm and steady focus on the project; Susan Lee, the editor, for her expertise, creativity, patience and unfailing good humour; and family members and friends for their encouragement and contributions.

The author and publisher would like to thank Paul Grover, Jane Curran and Roslyn Hayes for their detailed and helpful reviews of the manuscript. Their assistance is gratefully acknowledged.

The author and publisher would like to thank the following for granting permission to reproduce copyright material in this book.

Pictures
Australian Rugby Union/John Eales, p. 14; Fairfax Photo Library, pp. 19, 30, 35, 48, 103, 121 and 122; Image Network, Indonesia/Rio Helmi, pp. 128 and 129; Levi's Jeans, pp. 10 and 11; National Film and Sound Archive/Margaret Fink, pp. 56 and 57; John Shakespeare, p. 3; Sony, p. 26; Andrew Stark, p. 67; Sydney Freelance, pp. 6 (both), 36, 37, 39, 41 (all) and 45; TAFE NSW, p. 93; Triple J, p. 92; and R. M. Williams, p. 17.

Extracts
AusInfo/Legislative Services; Keith Austin; Linda Bruce; John Digby; Sarah Dinning; Steve Dow; Peter Fitzsimons; Jane Freeman; Michelle Gunn; Janet Hawley; 'Gifts', by Oodgeroo of the Tribe Noonuccal (formerly known as Kath Walker), in *My People 3rd edition*, 1990, published by Jacaranda Press; Dugald Jellie; Richard Jinman; Mark Juddery; Knight-Ridder/Tribune Information Services; Peter Kogoy; Elizabeth Lane; Sally Loane; Cassie McCullagh; Sacha Molitorisz; Mushroom Group of Companies; Pan Macmillan Australia Pty Ltd for the extract from *Secret Men's Business* by John Marsden, reprinted by permission, copyright (c) John Marsden 1998; Jim O'Rourke; Stephanie Peatling; Penguin Books Australia for the extracts from *Puberty Blues* by Kathy Lette and Gabrielle Carey and from *Seven Little Australians* by Ethel Turner; Cameron Sharp; Dale and Lynne Spender; *Rolling Stone*; Ruth Teale; The *Daily Telegraph*; The *Sun-Herald*; *TV Hits Magazine*; University of Queensland Press; Heather Vaile; and Jeremy Vincent.

Every effort has been made to trace and acknowledge copyright. The author and publisher would welcome any information from people who believe they own copyright to material in this book.

CONTENTS

ACKNOWLEDGMENTS		ii
INTRODUCTION		vii
ABOUT THE AUTHOR		vii
OUTCOMES		viii

chapter 1

image

1	**TRIBES** Sacha Molitorisz, 'Tribes of the city'	newspaper feature article	2
2	**LOVES OF THE LITERATI** Clarissa Bye, 'Loyalty is folly, says Gen X'	newspaper report	5
3	**THOSE CLOTHES!** Jim O'Rourke, 'All dressed down'	newspaper report	8
4	**THE LOOK** Levi's jeans	advertisements	9
5	**SEX APPEAL** Peter Fitzsimons, 'What a tangled web they weave to make rugby sexy'	newspaper report	13
6	**THE BUSH** Henry Lawson, 'Middleton's Rouseabout'	poem	15
7	**AUSSIE IMAGE** R. M. Williams boots	advertisement	16
8	**BEAUTY MYTHS** Cassie McCullagh, 'Object lesson'	magazine feature article	19
9	**ROSE-COLOURED DREAMS** Ethel Turner, *Seven Little Australians*	novel excerpt	21
Listening 10	**SWAMP RAT** Tim Winton, *Lockie Leonard, Human Torpedo*	novel excerpt	23

chapter 2

popular culture

1	**IF MUSIC BE…**		
	Sony	advertisement	26
	Elissa Blake, 'Various artists: Triple J Hottest 100 Vol. 5'	review	27
	Neil Finn (Crowded House), 'Don't Dream It's Over'	song lyric	29
2	**EVERYTHING OLD…**		
	Jeremy Vincent, 'Rebels without pause'	review	30
	Mark Juddery, 'A joyful, silly romp'	review	32
3	**HEROES AND IDOLS**		
	Andrew Humphreys, 'Hot idol: Lucy Lawless'	magazine feature article	34
	'Xenite hangouts'	infotainment	35
	Keith Austin, 'Schlock, battle and spice'	review	36
	Nicole Triantafillou, 'A brave walk on the wildside'	interview	38
4	**SPICE UP YOUR LIFE**		
	Tom Moon, 'Help wanted: no talent needed'	newspaper report	40
5	**TITANIC GAMES**		
	Linda Bruce, 'Disaster revisited'	review	42
	'20 fast facts: Leonardo DiCaprio'	infotainment	44
6	**SPONSORSHIP**		
	Adam Heimlich, 'The company they keep'	magazine feature article	46
7	**YOUNG FILM-MAKERS**		
	Richard Jinman, 'Teens turn the corner to film the nitty gritty'	newspaper report	48
Listening 8	**ROCK'N'ROLL**		
	Peter Goldsworthy, *Maestro*	novel excerpt	49

chapter 3

the opposite sex

1	**DIFFICULT KIDS**		
	William Shakespeare, *A Midsummer Night's Dream*	drama script	52
2	**AT THE BALL**		
	Eleanor Witcombe, *My Brilliant Career: The Screenplay*	film script	56
3	**A ROMANTIC LOVER**		
	Oodgeroo of the Tribe Noonuccal (formerly Kath Walker), 'Gifts'	poem	60
4	**FIRST LOVE**		
	Elizabeth Lane, *Mad as Rabbits*	autobiography	62
5	**THE END OF AN AFFAIR**		
	David Malouf, *Australian Autobiography*	autobiography	65
6	**FRIENDSHIP RINGS**		
	Kathy Lette and Gabrielle Carey, *Puberty Blues*	personal account	66

	7	**GENDER MATTERS**		
		Dale and Lynne Spender, 'Serial partners, multiple careers for the contemporary woman'	newspaper feature article	68
		Sally Loane, 'The trouble with boys'	newspaper feature article	72
Listening	8	**FIRST DATE DISASTER**		
		Melina Marchetta, *Looking for Alibrandi*	novel excerpt	75

chapter 4

careers

	1	**GREAT EXPECTATIONS**		
		Jane Freeman, 'Young dreams'	newspaper feature article	78
		'Pass with frying colours'	newspaper report	83
		Charles Dickens, *Great Expectations*	novel excerpt	84
	2	**SOME FACTS**		
		Labour force status and age—August 1997	dot graph	87
		Labour force participation rate, males and females—1982–97	line graph	87
		Employed persons, occupation—August 1997	information grid	87
	3	**OPTIONS**		
		TAFE NSW, *The Right Choice*	information report	88
	4	**DESPERATELY SEEKING…**		
		Australia Bank	advertisement	90
	5	**SUCCESS BY DEGREES**		
		University of Sydney, *Courses and Careers Day 1998*	information report	91
	6	**JOB ALERT**		
		'JobWatch'	information report	94
	7	**THE APPLICATION**		
		Lyndall Hough, Résumé preparation	instruction	96
	8	**TOADS**		
		Philip Larkin, 'Toads'	poem	98
Listening	9	**WORKWISE**		
		Face the panel	interviews	102

chapter 5

independence

	1	**ONE WAY OUT**		
		Steve Dow, 'Why children run away from home'	newspaper feature article	104
	2	**WAR**		
		Guy Edwards	letter	107
	3	**BREADWINNER**		
		Thomas Hardy, *Tess of the D'Urbervilles*	novel excerpt	109

	4	**OUTCAST**		
		Henry Fielding, *Tom Jones*	novel excerpt	112
	5	**GAY RIGHTS**		
		Cameron Sharp, *Hamilton High School Speech*	short story	114
	6	**IDENTITY CRISIS**		
		Michelle Gunn, 'Youth suffers identity crisis as rites of passage blur'	newspaper feature article	118
	7	**POLITICS**		
		Stephanie Peatling, 'PolitiKids'	newspaper feature article	120
Listening	8	**ON YOUR OWN**		
		School's out	presentation	124

chapter 6

choices

	1	**PRINCES AND PRINCESSES**		
		Ruth Trowbridge, 'Between the Lines'	poem	126
		Janet Hawley, 'The prince's bride'	magazine feature article	127
	2	**TRAVEL**		
		Australian passport application	form	131
		Dugald Jellie, 'Have visa, will work'	newspaper feature article	137
		Overseas student	letter	140
	3	**ISSUES AND OPINIONS**		
		Peter Kogoy, 'Teenagers say yes to sport drugs'	newspaper report	142
	4	**BELIEFS**		
		John Marsden, *Secret Men's Business*	self-help book excerpt	144
	5	**EVALUATION**		
		Peter Porter, 'A Consumer's Report'	poem	147
Listening	6	**ACROSS THE DESERT**		
		Robyn Davidson, *Tracks*	autobiography	149

APPENDIX: KEY TO TEXTS AND TERMS   151

INTRODUCTION

Between the Lines is designed to provide preparation for the New South Wales School Certificate English Literacy examination, which requires students to respond to a variety of types of text.

Activities in this book go beyond those required of the questioning in the School Certificate and, while they are not all typical of the examination, they will assist students to develop the skills they will need. For example, students have the opportunity to compose multiple-choice questions and listening tasks, which will help to give them a thorough understanding of the purpose of these types of activities.

The activities encourage students to extend their vocabulary skills, and dictionaries should be on hand at all times. Students will also need to use the appendix, which contains guidelines for composing various types of text and definitions of key terms for the study of English. Useful margin notes are also provided for many of the questions and activities. Each chapter includes a listening task.

Each chapter focuses on a theme and contains a selection of types of text, so that, overall, a comprehensive range is included. In addition to a variety of multimedia texts, the book includes a selection of literary texts, ranging from Shakespeare to popular contemporary writers.

The literary, factual and multimedia texts included are topical and challenging and will help students to develop their knowledge of the world about them. The texts in each chapter are of varying levels of difficulty and teachers should choose appropriate units of work for their classes. Teachers may also consider that the language of some texts needs modification for their particular classes.

Between the Lines could also be used as a language course book, an extension to a thematic unit of work and as a self-directed learning resource for organised and motivated students. There are also many activities designed for group work.

I hope the activities are useful and enjoyable for students and help busy teachers, who do not always have the time to find suitable material for class exercises and much less to create twenty or thirty practice questions.

Gillian Lovell

> Answers to select questions in this book are available in printed form on request. They can also be found on the Heinemann World Wide Web site: *hi.com.au/betweenthelines/*

about the AUTHOR

Gillian Lovell (MA Litt., Dip. Ed.) was Head of English at Meriden Girls' School for nine years. She is an experienced HSC marker and is now involved in curriculum development, writing and part-time teaching.

OUTCOMES

After studying the texts and completing the activities, students should be able to achieve the following outcomes.

reading and viewing

- understand and evaluate what they read and view in a wide range of contexts
- identify the distinguishing features of multimedia, factual and literary texts
- extend vocabulary skills in a wide range of contexts
- extend their comprehension beyond the literal to the inferential, creative, critical and analytical
- identify and discuss attitudes conveyed by written and visual texts
- identify the purpose, audience and situation of a range of texts
- engage in sustained, silent individual reading
- explain the effect of particular print styles, layouts, headings and illustrations and make judgments about their effectiveness
- explain the effect of visual material through its composition
- explore their reading through discussion, role play, debate and imaginative recreation
- research and explore new and unfamiliar reading and viewing materials

writing

- explain in both their own and others' writing the effects of purpose, content, audience and situation
- write for a variety of audience types and purposes
- edit and publish individual and group products for both limited and public audiences
- use writing to influence individuals, groups and situations
- use writing to record and arrange information from written, spoken or visual texts
- develop the ability to choose and shift register for particular situations and purposes

speaking and listening

- identify and explain the ways that purpose, audience and situation affect the register of speech
- engage in sustained discussion
- explore and analyse diverse literary and factual texts through talking and listening
- speak in a wide variety of formal and informal situations, using appropriate register
- evaluate the strengths and weaknesses of other speakers
- listen to spoken texts and identify content, purpose and tone

IMAGE

chapter 1

In this chapter you will be reading, viewing and listening to texts about 'image'—the image, or picture, we have of ourselves, the image we have of others and the different ways in which we try to create a particular image for a purpose.

As part of testing your literacy skills, you will be involved in group work as well as working on your own. You will be expanding your vocabulary and your knowledge of the key terms needed for the study of English.

You will be examining:
- newspaper and magazine articles
- newspaper reports
- advertisements
- novel excerpts
- a poem.

You will be finding out how and why they differ.

You will write:
- a diary entry
- a newspaper report
- an editorial
- a formal letter
- a speech
- a ballad.

You will be asked to design:
- a questionnaire
- a poster
- a pamphlet
- an advertisement.

By the end of this chapter, you should know much more about the type of language that is appropriate for these different text types.

1 **TRIBES**
Sacha Molitorisz
'Tribes of the city'

2 **LOVES OF THE LITERATI**
Clarissa Bye
'Loyalty is folly, says Gen X'

3 **THOSE CLOTHES!**
Jim O'Rourke
'All dressed down'

4 **THE LOOK**
Levi's jeans

5 **SEX APPEAL**
Peter Fitzsimons
'What a tangled web they weave to make rugby sexy'

6 **THE BUSH**
Henry Lawson
'Middleton's Rouseabout'

7 **AUSSIE IMAGE**
R. M. Williams boots

8 **BEAUTY MYTHS**
Cassie McCullagh
'Object lesson'

9 **ROSE-COLOURED DREAMS**
Ethel Turner
Seven Little Australians

10 Listening
SWAMP RAT
Tim Winton
Lockie Leonard, Human Torpedo

1 TRIBES

newspaper feature article

Sacha Molitorisz
'Tribes of the city'

People create an image of themselves when they choose to dress and/or behave in a particular way.

Tribes of the city

1   Young people today! Those clothes! That music! What do they think they look like? SACHA MOLITORISZ plunges deep into the urban jungle to identify and catalogue the latest stages in the evolution of the species.

2   As a teenager, your tribe is especially crucial: who you are is almost entirely determined by whether you play football or chess, heavy metal or classical. About the time you make the move from primary to high school, you suddenly realise it isn't cool to be like your parents. You don't want to belong to their generation, but you have to belong to something. So, as kids have done for decades, you adopt a look, a pastime, a lifestyle. You adopt a tribe.

3   In 1998, what are the predominant tribes? Actually, there are many, some exclusively for teens, others with members on the cusp of mid-life crisis. Today's youth can choose to join the Teenybopper ranks or instead give American culture a barely needed boost by becoming Homeboys and Homegirls; they can play the '90s game of being cool by being uncool as Web Geeks or Dorks; they can wear black and become Indie Kids; they can become Gothics or Yuppies, Bikies, Surfers or Skaters; if beer is their drug of choice they might become Lager Louts; if it's hallucinogens and crystals they might take the long and winding Crusty route; while the avowedly alternative might become Manga Kids or Ravers.

> We all do it. One way or another, we all join tribes.

4   These tribes might appear intimidating, but any old mod or rocker will tell you that cliques and gangs have existed for decades.

5   Still, the tribes of today are radically unlike those of, say, twenty years ago. First, understand that today's tribes are changing faster than ever. Our culture is increasingly about five-second sound bites and catering to diminishing attention spans. A tribe that is popular today may have disappeared next month.

6   Second, there are many more tribes and sub-tribes than ever before. The world is shrinking fast. A group of Tokyo teenagers might start aping a Japanese cartoon character, then set up a Web site to spread the word. Within days a group of kids in outback NSW might come across the site and adopt the same style.

7   Third, today's subcultures are often more mongrel than thoroughbred. In the '90s nothing is pure; people will dabble rather than immerse themselves, and the same is true of our tribes. Hence a Goth might also be a Web Geek, and a Skater might spend most of her time in the company of Ravers.

8   Fourth, in most cases, music is the defining element of a tribe. It often dictates how to dress, how to talk and how to behave.

9   With these thoughts in mind, let's stereotype ...

Street life

A SPOTTER'S GUIDE

HOMEBOYS/HOMEGIRLS Range from harmless teens in baggy pants, basketball singlets and caps (worn backwards, of course) to aggressive and obnoxious gangbangers who wield attitude, anger and spray cans. Homies walk and talk funny, as if they're auditioning for yet another rap music video. **Preferred habitat:** Campbelltown, Bankstown, Newtown.

TEENYBOPPERS A marketer's dream. TBs fall in love easily, usually with a pretty pop star (the Spice Girls; the Hanson bimbos) then buy said pop star's records, posters, T-shirts, socks and special limited edition personally autographed handkerchief boxed sets. Unimaginative and sheepish. Usually grow up to be prime ministers. **Preferred habitat:** everywhere.

DORKS In the '90s, the cult of irony rules. What used to be dorky is now ... well, still dorky ... but then, dorky is cool. Hence the body shirts, big collars, brown pants, manbags for him and sequins for her. An older, self-aware, occasionally pretentious subculture. **Preferred habitat:** Glebe, Newtown.

WEB GEEKS That's right, uncool is cool, and thus computer nerds have become fashion icons. Identifiable by bad dress sense, substandard social skills and puerile names: Phreaker, Mephisto, Nemo, etc. Few friends; fewer scruples; allergic to sunlight. Dangerous if competent enough to hack into the Pentagon. **Preferred habitat:** virtually everywhere.

INDIE KIDS Colour of wardrobe ranges extensively from black to noir. Feet: Doc Marten's. Bottom: Levi's (black). Top: T-shirt (black). Hair: anything goes, even colours. Most commonly found in cafés leafing through Sartre or Derrida and discussing the latest obscure alternative band. **Preferred habitat:** Surry Hills, Newtown.

YUPPIES They're loaded, they're amoral, and they're back. Step into a trendy CBD bar on a Thursday night (the Slip Inn, the Forbes, the Brooklyn) to see their mate-and-proliferate rituals. You know the look: imported suit, expensive car, designer sunglasses. Often prove the adage that money can't buy taste. **Preferred habitat:** CBD, Kirribilli (not Newtown).

GOTHS The tribe that never dies—maybe all that time spent loitering in graveyards yielded the secret of eternal life? Adherents look like extras from 'The Addams Family'. Nocturnal and not nearly as frightening as they seem. True Goths wake up two hours earlier than anyone else to apply make-up. **Preferred habitat:** Rockwood, Newtown.

BIKIES Perhaps the most resilient tribe of all, Harley-riding, denim-clad and tattoo-adorned. Congregate in gangs with scary names (Hell's Angels, Bandidos, etc.). Don't mess with. **Preferred habitat:** Liverpool, Newtown.

SURFIES Also long-lasting. Find them near any ocean beach, discussing the gnarly sets and wicked close-outs, dude. For male and female, hair must be blond and unkempt, skin must be freckly and salt-encrusted, eyes must be squinting and bloodshot (from seawater and illicit substances). Always barefoot. **Preferred habitat:** Beach suburbs.

SKATERS Into hardcore guitar bands (Sonic Youth, Mudhoney) and loitering at skate ramps (if one is available) or CBD buildings. Become panicky if separated from their boards for more than a few minutes. Recognise them by the scars on their knees and elbows. **Preferred habitat:** Bondi, Newtown.

LAGER LOUTS Imported from the UK, this male tribe is into ball games, beer and buddies. They wear Timberlands, jeans and a rugby jumper. Or, for formal occasions, Timberlands, jeans and a chambray shirt. Usually pre-yuppies with rich parents in the eastern suburbs, on the North Shore or in the country, would like to grow up to be Shane Warne; will grow up to be overweight. **Preferred habitat:** The Rocks, rugby clubs.

KOMBI-DRIVING CRUSTIES New Age hippies with no fixed address. They like crystals, peace and dreadlocks, dislike showers, authority and rego tests. They sprout from the ground in the verdant countryside in northern NSW before adopting a peripatetic existence in the hope of finding themselves. If you want to find them, just follow your nose. **Preferred habitat:** Nimbin to Newtown.

MANGA BOYS AND GIRLS These are the boys imitating Astro Boy and Akira (or at least wearing their T-shirt) and girls aspiring to be Aeon Flux or Sailor Venus. Manga Girls wear short skirts and bright T-shirts, Manga Boys wear coloured hair and snappy pants. **Preferred habitat:** Chinatown, Newtown.

RAVERS Some of the most exciting music of the moment is dance-based, so you'd expect there to be a thriving dance subculture. And there is, of which Ravers constitute the most conspicuous tribe. Ravers wear sneakers and fluorescent colours and hug anything that moves. Addicted to strobe lighting and repetitive beats, they go nowhere without a water bottle and a whistle. **Preferred habitat:** Warehouses, Newtown.

Sydney Morning Herald, 4 April 1998

BETWEEN THE LINES

1.1 In this question, all the suggested meanings of 'tribe' are correct, but which one fits best with what the writer goes on to say about tribes?

1.2 Questions about vocabulary usually suggest one or two meanings that are wrong, one or two that are close to being correct and could confuse you, and one that is the closest to the meaning of the word in its context. Sometimes the correct meaning is not easy to pick just by considering the context, so you need to develop your vocabulary skills.

1.3 A definition of 'tone' appears in the Key Terms section of the Appendix.

1.1 The word 'tribe', as it is used in the article, means:
 a any group of people united by ties of descent from a common ancestor
 b any group of people united by customs, traditions or behaviour
 c a social group that claims hunting rights in a particular area
 d a company, troop or number of persons or animals.

1.2 The word closest in meaning to 'intimidating' (paragraph 4) is:
 a boring
 b new
 c frightening
 d impressive.

1.3 In about five or six lines, explain how the writer creates a conversational tone.

1.4 In paragraph 5 the writer states 'the tribes of today are radically unlike those of, say, twenty years ago.' In your own words, summarise the four reasons given for this (see the margin note on page 5).

1.5 'More mongrel than thoroughbred' (paragraph 7) in this context means:
   a mixed rather than pure
   b dog-like
   c not of the best blood
   d more aggressive than gentle.

1.6 'Let's stereotype' (paragraph 9) suggests that the writer is going to:
   a listen to what the tribes say
   b make a mould
   c describe people
   d put people in categories.

1.7 In paragraph 2 and the Street Life section the writer comments on the tribes as though they are animals. What gives this impression? Explain your reasons in about ten or twelve lines.

1.8 Fourteen tribes are described in the Street Life section and each is represented by a cartoon. Research the meaning of 'cartoon' and discuss why cartoons might have been chosen to illustrate the article. Do you think they are effective? How else may the writer have chosen to illustrate the article? Write about ten to twelve lines explaining your opinion.

1.9 Writing
Choose one of the categories mentioned in the Street Life section and write a diary entry covering a day in the life of a person belonging to that category. Write about a page.

1.10 Writing
Divide into pairs or small groups and choose a 'tribe' from the Street Life section. Study the tribe's description and the matching cartoon. Research any words or phrases that you don't understand and then write a conversation between two members of the tribe. Role play your conversations for the class.

1.4 Refer to the Appendix for guidelines on summaries.

Dictionaries should be on hand at all times.

2 LOVES of the literati

Clarissa Bye
'Loyalty is folly, says Gen X'

newspaper report

One particular generation of young people is having a profound influence on all sorts of products. It is Generation X, and the choices they make contribute to their image.

Loyalty is folly, says Gen X

By CLARISSA BYE Social Affairs Reporter

1. THEY use products from The Body Shop, watch 'Seinfeld' and 'The Simpsons' and their favourite brands include Nike, Calvin Klein and Levi's.

2. Introducing the Literati, the latest social group to be targeted by advertisers. They are aged between eighteen and thirty, and are the most savvy generation yet. A steady diet of advertising and media analysis means they view marketing as a game.

3. Traditional heroes are out, while those who display a weakness or vulnerability—such as cricketer Mark Taylor, who kept his chin up during a form slump—are preferred. Their favourite advertisements are those of Smirnoff, Sony, McDonald's and Libra.

4. Sydney research firm Heartbeat has just released a new social research tool—an interactive CD-ROM based on focus groups—into the generation that reached adulthood in the '90s.

5. Research director Rob Marjenberg said the twenty-somethings investigated every brand that came their way, digging for the truth beneath the image.

6. 'Everyone talks about how advertising-literate this generation is,' Mr Marjenberg said.

7. 'They have grown up with advertising; when it comes to marketing they are incredibly fine-tuned.'

8. He said that was why The Body Shop had emerged as a new type of brand for the '90s. 'We found that The Body Shop is seen as a brand that is willing to stand up for what it believes in—the environment, fairness, society—and actually does something about it,' he said.

9. Heartbeat managing director Jem Wallis said the Literati was profoundly sceptical and disillusioned with big business.

10. 'In their eyes, loyalty is folly and trust is naive,' Mr Wallis said. 'For them, self-reliance is the key. They are the do-it-yourself generation.'

11. Many dream to 'beat the system'—striking out on their own, outside the established structure. 'Ideally for many that means setting up their own business where they have a sense of control, security and independence,' Mr Wallis said.

12. 'They want to work without chains.'

13. The researchers said the generation often rejected icons that seemed ideal, instead searching out the human behind the veneer.

14. Heroes were as diverse as South African President Nelson Mandela, actor Nicole Kidman and rugby league star Paul Harragon.

15. 'They do not suffer phoneys,' the researchers reported. 'They are generally sceptical of the establishment. They like to dig below the surface to see what is really there. They do not see this as cynical, just astute.

16. 'Alanis Morissette may sing of pain, but her message is positive. She is together and in control.

17. 'Nicole Kidman is an Aussie girl made good, but above all else her family seems to be her priority and she is loyal to husband Tom Cruise and to her own parents.'

Sun Herald, 8 March 1998

LOVES OF THE LITERATI

TOP TV SHOWS
Seinfeld
Friends
The Simpsons
The X Files

TOP HEROES
Alanis Morissette
Mark Taylor
Nicole Kidman
Paul Harragon

TOP ADS
Smirnoff
Sony
McDonald's
Libra

TOP BRANDS
The Body Shop
Nike
Calvin Klein
Levi's

BETWEEN THE LINES

2.1 In groups, research the meaning of 'loyalty' and 'folly' and make up a multiple-choice question about the meaning of the headline. Pass the questions around the groups, and discuss and peer assess the suggestions.

2.1 Refer to the Appendix for guidelines on multiple-choice questions.

2.2 In groups, discuss the purpose of the graphic. Write five or six lines explaining whether or not you think it is effective.

2.3 Research the dictionary meaning of 'literati' and then reread paragraphs 2, 6 and 7. Write a definition of 'literati' as it is used in this report. What is the connection between the 'literati' and 'Gen (Generation) X' referred to in the headline?

2.4 In groups, research the meaning of the following words used in this report: 'savvy' (paragraph 2), 'vulnerability' (paragraph 3), 'sceptical' and 'disillusioned' (paragraph 9), 'naive' (paragraph 10) 'icons' and 'veneer' (paragraph 13), 'phoneys', 'cynical' and 'astute' (paragraph 15) and 'priority' (paragraph 17).

Rewrite the sentences in which they occur, substituting another word or phrase. Make sure the sentences still make sense when you have rewritten them.

2.4 Refer to margin note 1.2 (p. 4).

2.5 'Traditional heroes are out, while those who display a weakness or vulnerability... are preferred' (paragraph 3). The report suggests that traditional heroes are:
   a not popular because they cannot cope with form slumps
   b always strong and unlikely to be hurt in any way
   c likely to let their chins drop
   d seen as having an unrealistic veneer of strength.

2.5 This question depends on your ability to work out what is being inferred or suggested by the writer. You are not given a definition of traditional heroes, so you need to work out what they are by analysing the description of the preferred type of hero.

2.6 Rob Marjenberg said that 'when it comes to marketing they [the literati] are incredibly fine-tuned' (paragraph 7). He means that:
   a the literati know what to sell at the markets
   b they are tuned to the right stations
   c the literati are experienced and discerning consumers
   d they know what music they want.

2.7 The Body Shop is popular because it:
   a is a new brand
   b is an organisation with a social conscience
   c promotes a better body
   d takes action on important social issues.

2.8 Write ten to twelve lines on the qualities of the literati.

2.9 Writing
In groups, design a questionnaire for the students in your year (or another year) to find out their favourite products, television shows, films and heroes. Using the results of your research, write a newspaper report or feature article on your findings. Include a visual representation in the form of a picture or graph.

2.9 Refer to the Appendix for guidelines on newspaper reports and feature articles.

IMAGE 7

3 those CLOTHES!

newspaper report

Jim O'Rourke
'All dressed down'

How people dress projects a very strong image of who they are, what they do and how they behave, so employers are often fussy about the appearance of their employees.

All dressed down

1 Centrelink workers told jeans are out and uniforms are in.
By JIM O'ROURKE Workplace Reporter

2 PUBLIC servants at the former Department of Social Security are to be banned from wearing jeans and runners because customers said the workers were too scruffy.

3 Staff at Centrelink offices will have to wear either a specially designed corporate uniform—which they have to pay for—or clothing deemed by management to be of a similar standard.

4 Even workers who never deal personally with the public will not be allowed to wear jeans in the office. Staff who fail to meet the standards will face disciplinary action, including being sent home to change and having wages docked for the time spent away from their desks.

5 Centrelink management said it surveyed its clients—people who receive unemployment, family and other benefits—who reported that the professionalism of the organisation was judged on the appearance of its staff.

6 Other clothing deemed inappropriate under the 'minimum standard of dress' policy includes items with political, commercial or religious messages, football shorts and stubbies, bike pants, midriff tops and flanelette shirts.

7 The infamous 1970s-style footwear, the Ugg boot, is also banned.

8 Workers will be allowed to wear jeans which are 'tidy and in proper repair' during a six-month transitional period ending on 31 July.

9 The Community and Public Sector Union claimed the dress code came as service levels at Centrelink were being affected by staff levels which were at an all-time low.

10 Union assistant State secretary Sharon Draper said staff were angry that respectable work attire, such as neat and tidy jeans, would be banned.

11 'We have no argument with management that our members should be presentable, clean, neat and tidy when at work or dealing with the public,' Ms Draper said.

12 'But Centrelink is not being flexible by banning jeans and runners from the workplace.

13 'Jeans and clean runners are worn by people to nightclubs and expensive restaurants, why not at work?

14 'People who work in backroom operations, away from the public, should be allowed to wear comfortable casual clothing.'

15 Ms Draper said management was encouraging people to buy the corporate uniform even though some workers on junior ranks would find it difficult to afford.

16 She said women, for example, had to pay $60 for a blouse bearing the Centrelink logo—an item of clothing they could not wear away from the workplace.

17 'The union is not insisting our members parade around in flannelette shirts and shorts,' she said.

18 'They are not stupid, they know what clothing is inappropriate to the workplace.'

19 A Centrelink spokesman spokesman said most staff members were in favour of the minimum dress standards.

EDITORIAL: Page 48.

Sun Herald, 8 March 1998

BETWEEN THE LINES

3.1 A public servant (paragraph 2) is:
  a someone who has to serve someone else
  b a person employed by the government
  c an employee of a public-owned company
  d a maid employed at Government House.

Write short answers (about three to four lines) to questions and activities 3.2 to 3.8.

3.2 What is the newspaper report about?

3.3 Why is the dress code changing for Centrelink staff?

3.4 List the items of clothing that are considered inappropriate.

3.5 What is the response of the Community and Public Sector Union to the new dress code?

3.6 Mention TWO points that the Union spokesperson, Ms Draper, makes about the dress code.

3.7 Find out the colloquial meaning of 'a dressing down' and then explain the meaning of the headline 'All dressed down'.

3.8 How do you know this is a newspaper report? List all the features of a newspaper report that are evident in the story.

> **3.8** Refer to the Appendix for guidelines on newspaper reports before answering this question.

3.9 Writing
At the end of the newspaper report, you see printed 'EDITORIAL: Page 48'.
   Write the editorial, clearly expressing your opinion on the topic that jeans and runners should be banned for all workers. Remember to give your editorial an interesting headline.

> **3.9** Refer to the Appendix for guidelines on writing an editorial.

4 the LOOK

Levi's jeans
girls' jeans (a) and boys' jeans (b)

A particular image is often used to sell a product. McDonald's has long used the image of fun and smiling friendliness to sell its product, while Levi's has adopted a very different image for its world-famous jeans.

advertisements

a BETWEEN THE LINES

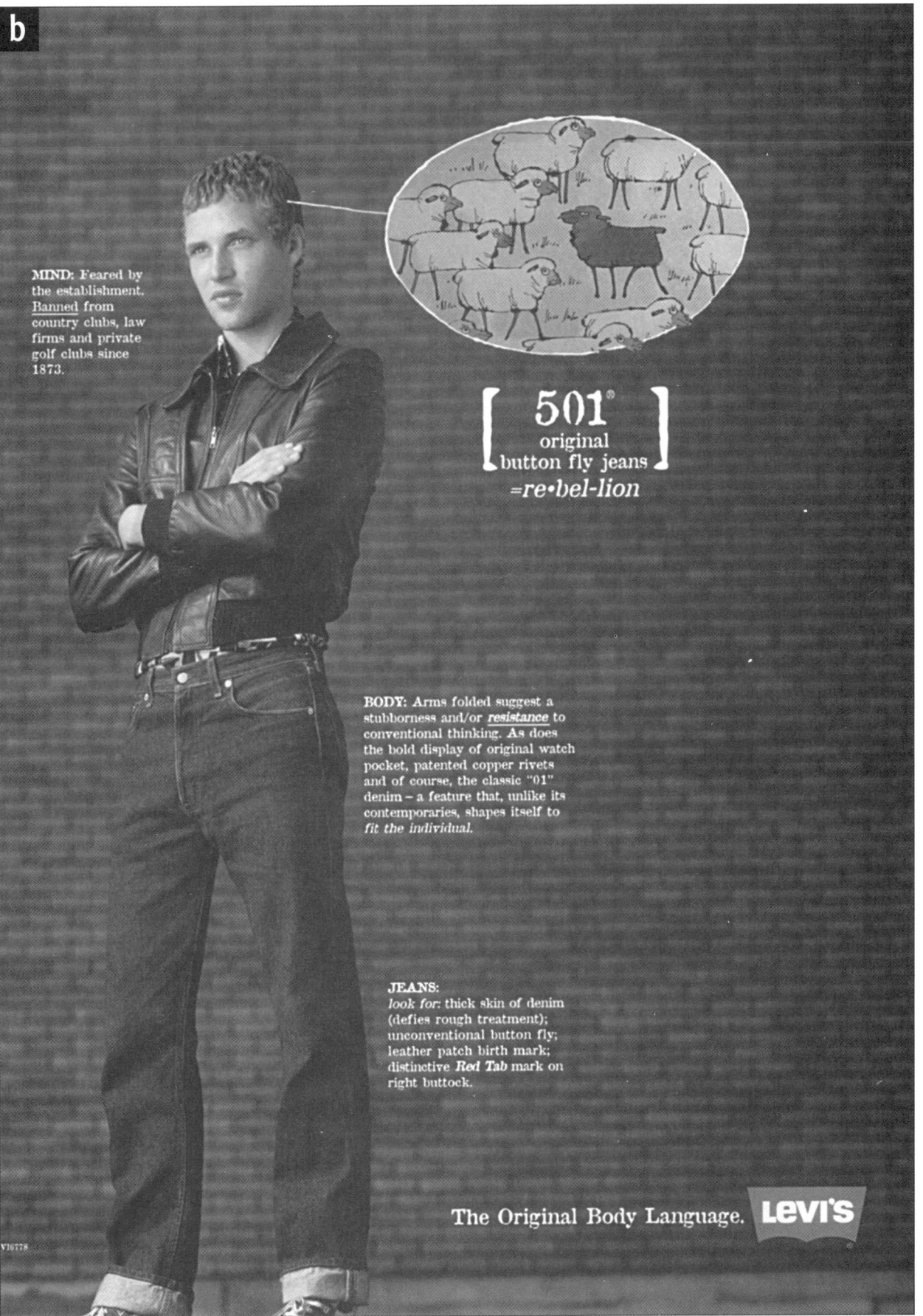

BETWEEN THE LINES

Study advertisement (a) before responding to questions and activities 4.1 to 4.6.

4.1 The image of young women suggested by the picture of the girl is:
   a aggressive
   b rebellious
   c uncompromising
   d all of the above.

4.2 This image is used because:
   a this is an advertisement
   b Levi's jeans are tough and uncompromising
   c Levi's is linking a particular image with its jeans
   d young women who wear these jeans have more fun.

4.3 The terms MIND, BODY and JEANS are presented as entries in a dictionary because:
   a this suggests an authoritative definition
   b it's easy to refer to and read
   c the definitions suggest the character of '501 woman'
   d '501 woman' cannot talk in sentences.

4.4 Study the text of the advertisement. Choose TWO words used in the text and explain how they suggest both the attitude of the girl and the quality of the jeans.

4.5 Comment on how the other clothing the girl is wearing adds to the impact of the advertisement.

4.6 Explain the point of the illustration in the balloon. Write about six to eight lines.

Study advertisement (b) before responding to questions and activities 4.7 and 4.8.

4.7 Explain the metaphor referred to in the balloon.

4.8 How is the metaphor continued in the advertisement? Consider the text (for example 'resistance to conventional thinking' and 'unconventional') and the visual features (for example the way the boy is standing).

4.9 What do you think 'The Original Body Language' means?

4.10 Compare the composition of the two advertisements. In what ways is the composition of each advertisement the same? In what ways is the composition of each advertisement different?

4.11 Writing
Write a formal letter to the Advertising Manager of Levi's. In your letter you should comment on the use and success of the advertisements. Begin your letter with 'Dear Sir/Madam'. Write about 300 to 400 words.

4.7 A definition of 'metaphor' appears in the Key Terms section of the Appendix.

4.10 Before completing this task, refer to the Appendix for guidelines on analysing visual texts. Pay particular attention to the background shade (light or dark), the shades used for the boy and the girl, the position of the main figures, the angle they are viewed from and their body language and facial expressions.

4.11 Refer to the Appendix for guidelines on argument and formal letters.

5 sex APPEAL

Peter Fitzsimons
'What a tangled web they weave to make rugby sexy'

newspaper report

The Australian Rugby Union team is attempting to sell its product as an entertaining game by adopting an image. In this case, each player is depicted as an animal. The strength and beauty of the animals are supposed to be attractive and 'sexy'.

BETWEEN THE LINES

Read the report on page 14 and then complete the following questions and activities.

5.1 Refer to the margin to find the origin of the headline. Explain the allusion and why it is particularly appropriate in this case.

> **5.1** 'O what a tangled web we weave,
> When first we practise to deceive!'
> Sir Walter Scott, *Marmion*, VI

5.2 The writer's attitude is:
   a enthusiastic
   b sceptical
   c objective
   d highly critical.

> **5.1** An allusion is a reference to another piece of writing, a legend, an event or another person.

5.3 John Eales is depicted as a spider because:
   a he is a large and frightening man
   b he has long legs like a spider
   c it is difficult to get the ball past him
   d he has a web around him.

5.4 The word 'charisma' (paragraph 9) means:
   a the personal qualities of a person
   b the ability to influence and impress people
   c the sex appeal that some people have
   d the sort of glamour celebrities have.

5.5 Eales thinks the campaign is good because:
   a he was happy to be a spider
   b girls will be attracted to him
   c it will sell the game of rugby
   d he could keep his clothes on.

5.6 Study the photograph. Decide whether you think the advertising campaign is a success. Justify your opinion in about five or six lines.

> **5.6** Refer to the Appendix for guidelines on analysing visual texts.

5.7 Writing
   In groups, plan an advertising and publicity campaign to promote attendance at the school's sports day. Design posters and a pamphlet. Peer assess the presentations.

What a tangled web they weave to make rugby sexy

By PETER FITZSIMONS

Wallaby skipper John Eales as the spider.

1. SEX appeal, that's what the game needs. So what do they do? They get a photographer to turn the Australian Rugby Union captain, John Eales, into a spider.
2. Yeah, right! Really sexy.
3. As Eales confided yesterday: 'I was just happy I could keep my clothes on.'
4. Which is more than his teammate, half-back George Gregan, managed to do when he posed for rugby's latest promotional campaign—a series of photos that bring out the animal in the game's stars.
5. Gregan, in an earlier shoot, was required to strip down to be portrayed as a cheetah at lethal full stretch.
6. Fullback Matthew Burke is depicted as a vulture sitting on the cross-bars, ready to swoop, in the campaign by the Leo Burnett, Connaghan and May Advertising Agency. But Eales as a spider?
7. 'That's the way we saw him,' says the agency's creative director, Nick Souter. 'This massive, athletic man, in the line-out and everywhere, whom it is just impossible to get a ball past. It's like he always has this enormous web around him.
8. 'Not everyone will like it, perhaps, but we think most will. Rugby has this image of being a bit stuffy, just for private school boys, and we're trying to make it more accessible and interesting to everyone, highlighting its strengths.'
9. Souter is endeavouring 'to create stars within the game, to lend some celebrity charisma to it and give it glamour and sex appeal'.
10. The photographer, Simon Harsent, was flown back from New York last week to complete the series. The Eales shoot took only a few hours, though the construction of the spider suit took several weeks.
11. Speaking from Durban yesterday, Eales said: 'I think the campaign is a good thing because it attracts attention to rugby, and I was happy to play my part in that.
12. 'I might say, though, that I'm not personally convinced on the sex appeal thing, especially when you think that of all the creatures in the world, the *least* attractive to women is spiders.'
13. Down came a spider and sat down beside her ...
14. Ah, what a tangled web they weave.

Sydney Morning Herald,
2 May 1998

6 the BUSH

Henry Lawson
'Middleton's Rouseabout'

poem

An image is often associated with a particular nationality, area or job. In Australia, we have an image of the bushman as rugged, hardworking and loyal to his mates. This image has been created through the stories and poems of Australian writers and is sometimes referred to as the 'bush tradition'.

> Tall and freckled and sandy,
> Face of a country lout;
> This was the picture of Andy,
> Middleton's Rouseabout.
>
> 5 Type of a coming nation,
> In the land of cattle and sheep,
> Worked on Middleton's station,
> 'Pound a week and his keep'.
>
> On Middleton's wide dominions
> 10 Plied the stockwhip and shears;
> Hadn't any opinions,
> Hadn't any 'idears'.
>
> Swiftly the years went over,
> Liquor and drought prevailed;
> 15 Middleton went as a drover
> After his station had failed.
>
> Type of a careless nation,
> Men who are soon played out,
> Middleton was:—and his station
> 20 Was bought by the Rouseabout.
>
> Flourishing beard and sandy,
> Tall and solid and stout;
> This is the picture of Andy,
> Middleton's Rouseabout.
>
> 25 Now on his own dominions
> Works with his overseers;
> Hasn't any opinions,
> Hasn't any idears.
>
> *Penguin Book of Australian Verse*, 1976

BETWEEN THE LINES

6.1 Find out what a 'rouseabout' is.

6.2 'Type of a coming nation' means that:
  a the nation was on the move
  b Andy was typical of workers developing a new country
  c the area was a type of country
  d everyone was tall, freckled and sandy.

6.3 Write a short description of Andy in your own words.

6.4 'Idears' (line 12) is in inverted commas in the poem because:
  a Henry Lawson has misspelled the word by mistake
  b 'idears' has a different meaning from 'ideas'
  c Andy cannot spell
  d it sounds the way Andy said it.

> **6.5 AND 6.6**
> These types of questions are called 'cloze' questions. Copy out the sentences and fill in the missing words after careful study of the material.

6.5 Middleton could not keep his station because of drought and _____ . He finally left and became a _____ . Henry Lawson suggests that Middleton was _____ .

6.6 Finally, Andy saves enough _____ to _____ the station (refer to lines 19–20). While he is still described as _____ and _____ , he now has a _____ and is _____ and _____ (refer to lines 1–4 and 21–4).

> **6.7** A definition of 'irony' appears in the Key Terms section of the Appendix.

6.7 In groups, discuss what you think lines 25–8 mean. Is Henry Lawson using irony, suggesting that Andy did have opinions and ideas, or is he suggesting that Andy was likely to repeat his boss's mistakes? Remember to use the whole poem to form your opinion. Write an answer in about ten or twelve lines.

> **6.8** 'Images' include people, landscapes and situations.

6.8 In groups, make a collage of advertisements that use images from the bush to sell a product.

6.9 Writing
Write a short ironic piece (about eight or ten lines) based on a situation at school, at home or at work.

7 AUSSIE image

advertisement

R. M. Williams boots

This advertisement appeals to our loyalty to Australia and draws on images of the bush tradition.

Australian boots should be Australian made.

    They make our running shoes in countries
where you've barely room to walk, and
they say that it's designed to increase trade.
They make our boomerangs in China
5 and umbrellas in Tibet.
But Australian boots should be Australian made.

    They make our cricket bats in Pakistan,
computers in Taiwan.
Some day soon they'll make pavlovas in Nepal.
10 The French make love, they reckon,
like no other race on earth,
and the English don't make very much at all.

    But it's when you're on a stock horse,
in the heat and dust and dirt,
15 and you know that you're a five-day ride from town.
You're depending on the boots you wear
to last through thick and thin.
You have to know those boots won't let you down.

    And you hope the bloke who made them
20 made real sure that not one stitch
will tear, come loose or somehow get all frayed.
That's the time you won't begrudge the fact
you paid a little more,
for Australian boots, that are Australian made.

THE BUSHMEN'S OUTFITTER

Boots and All

AUSTRALIAN MADE • AUSTRALIAN OWNED

Adelaide • Sydney • Melbourne • Brisbane • Perth
Canberra • Toowoomba • London • Auckland • Christchurch

BETWEEN THE LINES

7.1 Refer to the Appendix for guidelines on analysing visual texts before completing this activity.

7.1 Write a paragraph about the image of the bushman in the photograph.

7.2 The designer of the advertisement decided to include a ballad because:
   a people may remember it better
   b Australian bush ballads are famous
   c bush ballads reflect the Aussie image
   d all of the above.

7.3 Definitions of 'irony' and 'metaphor' appear in the Key Terms section of the Appendix.

7.3 'They make our running shoes in countries / where you've barely room to walk' (lines 1 and 2) is an example of:
   a humour
   b stupidity
   c irony
   d a metaphor.

7.4 Find an example of irony in the first twelve lines and write about ten lines explaining your choice.

7.5 'The English don't make very much at all' (line 12) is a remark that:
   a belittles the English because they don't make love
   b is a statement of fact about the English
   c is an example of the Australian jokes about 'Poms'
   d belittles the English because they don't sell anything.

7.6 Lines 13–24 focus on:
   a working conditions
   b the person who makes boots
   c the cost of the boots
   d the qualities of the boots.

7.7 The phrase 'won't begrudge' (line 22) means will not:
   a be contented about
   b be discontented about
   c be pleased about
   d shout about.

7.8 What is the purpose of repetition in the ballad?

7.9 Why do the words 'Boots and All' appear at the end of the advertisement? Research the usual meaning of the expression. Explain the literary device or technique being used here.

7.10 A definition of 'colloquial language' appears in the Key Terms section of the Appendix.

7.10 Write down three examples of Australian colloquial language used in the ballad.

7.11 In groups, research Australian bush ballads in the library. Prepare a presentation on the features of ballads and illustrate it by a group performance of a ballad or extracts from more than one ballad.

7.12 Writing

Plan a speech in which you argue for or against the following statement: 'The bush tradition is only one part of the Australian image.' Peer assess the speeches by presenting them in class.
OR
Write your own ballad. Peer assess the ballads through class performance.

> **7.12** Refer to the Appendix for guidelines on argument and speech.

8 BEAUTY myths

Cassie McCullagh
'Object lesson'

magazine feature article

We are often manipulated into adopting a certain image in the hope that it will make us more attractive to someone else or that we will feel more powerful and confident.

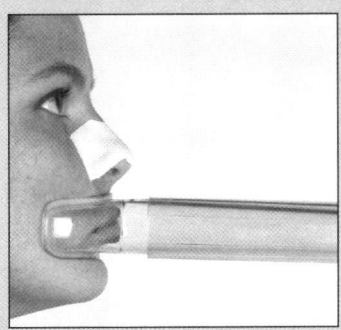
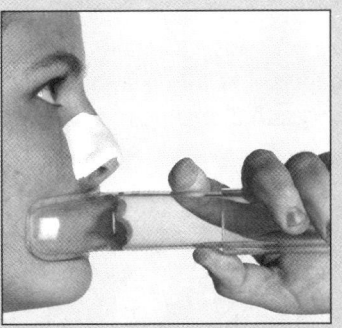

Object lesson

Anyone who has stood in front of a bathroom mirror knows the fun to be had in squeezing, popping, picking and pulling. Fun means money, and canny marketers are capitalising on our taste for do-it-yourself, soft-core cosmetic surgery. Even if you haven't heard of Biore Pore Pack, chances are that before long you'll have one plastered to your
5   nose. The 'deep-cleansing strip', which hardens on a wet nose and is then peeled off with a small forest of, ahem, 'impurities' attached, is big news in the beauty industry. Since Biore's arrival in Australia in September, product manager Anthony O'Brien says the response has been 'phenomenal'. Clearly he is hoping for sales similar to those in Japan where, he claims, 36 million packets were sold in the first year.
10   Also capitalising on our taste for DIY cosmetic surgery is Facial Sculpturing Inc., whose Lip Enhancer promises 'sexy full lips in seconds'. The pump-action cylinder and mouthpiece is said to draw the mouth into a perky pout for up to eight hours. Although initial use may cause bruising and discolouration (and pain, said our tester), continued use is claimed to increase fullness of the lips 'without spending thousands on surgery or
15   collagen implants.' But are these products good for you? Dr David Wong, honorary secretary of the Australasian College of Dermatologists, says the pore strips are only a temporary solution to the problem of blackheads and, as the process probably takes off a layer of skin, the risk of spreading infection is increased and the nose is left more sun-sensitive. Somewhat bemused by the claims made for the lip enhancer, he suggests
20   that prolonged use could actually create more lines. 'You're irritating the lips to cause inflation, which ultimately must leave them more lax.'

– Cassie McCullagh

Good Weekend, 7 February 1998

BETWEEN THE LINES

8.1 'Canny marketers' (line 2) are those who:
   a sell beauty products
   b are clever and shrewd salespeople
   c can make beauty products
   d like making money.

8.2 'Soft-core cosmetic surgery' (line 3) is:
   a cosmetic surgery that is easy to perform
   b a do-it-yourself beauty aid
   c simple cosmetic surgery you can carry out yourself
   d a soft instrument for altering the shape of your lips.

8.3 In the phrase 'a small forest of, ahem, "impurities" attached' (line 6), 'ahem' is used because it:
   a is related to the metaphor of forests
   b shows the writer wants to use a word that is an alternative to pimples
   c is a precise, technical, medical term
   d is naturally used in conversational language.

8.4 'Capitalising on our taste for DIY cosmetic surgery' (line 10) means:
   a taking advantage of people's liking for products that they can use themselves to improve their appearance
   b taking advantage of people's taste for products that improve their appearance
   c people prefer cosmetics that they can apply themselves
   d taking advantage of people's need for cosmetic surgery.

8.5 The long-term disadvantage of the Lip Enhancer is that it:
   a may cause bruising and discolouration
   b may cause more lines
   c irritates the lips
   d softens the lips.

> **8.6** Refer to the Appendix for guidelines on analysing visual texts.

8.6 Do you think the photographs of the model using the Lip Enhancer and Biore Pore pack are effective? Why or why not? Are they suitable illustrations for this article? Explain the reasons for your opinion in about eight to ten lines. Before writing your answer, make notes on Cassie McCullagh's attitude to the products, her purpose in writing this article and the impact of the photographs.

> **8.7** Refer to the Appendix for guidelines on reviews.

8.7 Writing
Design an advertisement for the Lip Enhancer for a teenagers' magazine, a newspaper, or for television or radio. Be careful to include the information in the article.
OR
Choose a product, real or imaginary, and write a review of its advantages and disadvantages.

9 rose-coloured DREAMS

Ethel Turner
Seven Little Australians

novel excerpt

There is nothing new about using beauty products to try to make ourselves look more attractive. Read the account from a novel published in 1894, more than 100 years ago.

> 'She is not yet so old
> But she may learn: happier than this,
> She is not bred so dull but she can learn.'

1   Meg's hair had always been pretty, but during the last two months she had cut herself a fringe, and begun to torture it up in curl papers every night. And in her private drawer she kept a jam tin filled with oatmeal, that she used in the water every time she
5   washed, having read it was a great complexion beautifier. And nightly she rubbed vaseline on her hands and slept in old kid gloves. And her spare money went in the purchase of 'Freckle Lotion', to remove that slight powdering of warm brown sun-kisses that somehow lent a certain character to her face.
10   All these things were the outcome of being sixteen, and having found a friend of seventeen.
    Aldith MacCarthy learnt French from the same teacher that Meg was going to twice a week, and after an exchange of chocolates, hair-ribbons, and family confidences a friendship sprang up.
15   Aldith had three grown-up sisters, whom she aped in everything, and was considerably wiser in the world than simple-minded, romantic Meg.
    She lent Meg novels, *Family Herald Supplements*, *Young Ladies' Journals*, and such publications, and the young girl took to them
20   with avidity, surprised at the new world into which they took her; for Charlotte Yonge and Louisa Alcott and Miss Wetherall had hitherto formed her simple and wholesome fare.
    Meg began to dream rose-coloured dreams of the time when her fair, shining hair should be gathered up into 'a simple knot at the
25   back of her head' or 'brushed into a regal coronet', these being the styles in which the heroines in the novels invariably dressed their hair. A pigtail done in three was very unromantic. That was why, as a sort of compromise, she cut herself a fringe and began to frizz out the end of her plait. Her father stared at her, and said she looked
30   like a shop-girl, when first he noticed it, and Esther told her she was a stupid child; but the looking-glass and Aldith reassured her.
    The next thing was surreptitiously to lengthen her dresses, which were at the short-long stage. In the privacy of her own bedroom she

took the skirts of two or three of her frocks off the band, inserted a piece of lining for lengthening purposes, and then added a frill to the waists of her bodices to hide the join. This dropped the skirts a good two inches, and made her look quite a tall, slim figure, as she was well aware.

And none of these things were very harmful.

But Aldith gradually grew dissatisfied with her waist.

'You're at least twenty-three, Marguerite,' she said once, quite in a horrified way.

She never called her friend Meg, pronouncing that name to be 'too domestic and altogether unlovely'.

Meg glanced from her own waist to her friend's slender, beautiful one, and sighed profoundly.

'What ought I to be?' she said in a low tone; and Aldith had answered, 'Eighteen—or nineteen, Marguerite, at the most; true symmetrical grace can never be obtained with a waist twenty-three inches round.'

Aldith had not only made statements and comparisons, she had given her friend practical advice, and shown her how the thing was to be done. And every night and morning Meg pulled away ruthlessly at her corset laces, and crushed her beautiful little body into narrower space. She had already brought it within a girdle of twenty-one inches, which was a clear saving of two, and she had taken in all her dresses at the seams.

But she gave up the evening game of cricket, and she never made one at rounders now, much to the others' disgust. No one, to look at the sweet blossomlike face, and soft, calm eyes, could have guessed what torture was being felt beneath the now pretty, well-fitting dress body. To walk quickly was positive pain; to stoop, almost agony; but she endured it all with a heroism worthy of a truly noble cause.

BETWEEN THE LINES

9.1 The extract of poetry at the beginning of the novel excerpt means she:
   a is old, but will probably learn
   b is young and intelligent enough to learn
   c will be happier and wiser if she learns
   d is young and, better, intelligent enough to learn.

9.2 List the words and phrases that show Ethel Turner's criticism of Meg's beauty routines.

9.3 List the words and phrases that show Turner's attitude towards Meg and towards Aldith. What is Turner's attitude to each girl? Write about twelve lines. Be sure to support your opinion with evidence from the extract.

9.4 Writing

Continue the story to explain what happens as a result of Meg wearing corsets. Remember to adapt your language and expression to the appropriate style. Write about 400 to 500 words.

OR

Make a list of the methods we use now to make ourselves attractive, for example cosmetic surgery and ear and navel piercing. Choose one method and adapt this story from *Seven Little Australians* for the present day.

listening

10 SWAMP rat

Tim Winton
Lockie Leonard, Human Torpedo

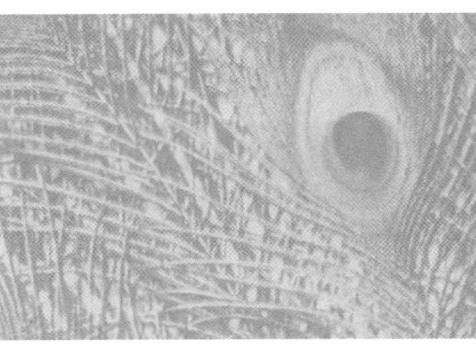

novel excerpt

Often when we are attracted to someone else, we are desperate to make a good impression. It is usually a disaster.

BETWEEN THE LINES

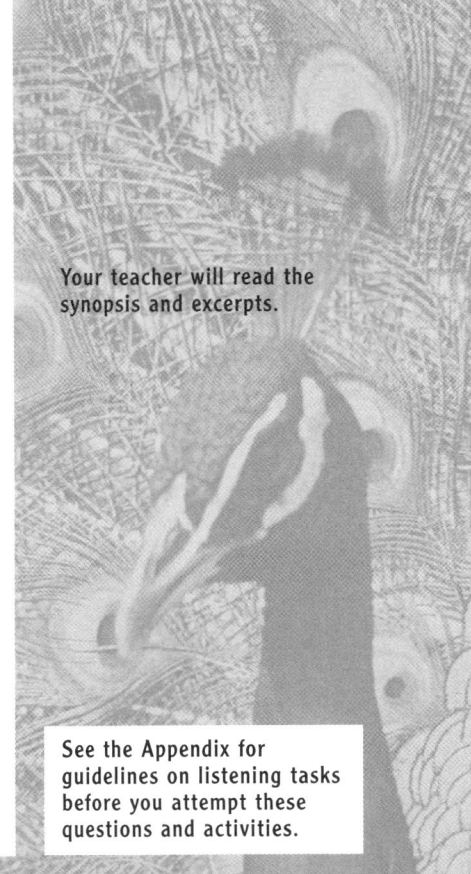

Your teacher will read the synopsis and excerpts.

Lockie and his family move to a small coastal town where Lockie's father is the Sergeant of Police. Their house is on swampy ground in the worst street in town and Lockie is immediately nicknamed Swamp Rat. At school he meets Vicki Streeton, whose parents run a successful business. He falls instantly in love with Vicki and feels the need to impress her. His chance comes when he is invited to go water-skiing. Although he is an excellent and keen surfboard rider, he has never been on water-skis...

The teacher will read an excerpt from the chapter headed Swamp Rat, starting on page 81 with 'Vicki streaked out in a long, sweeping fan of water' and ending on page 83 with 'She gave him a queer look. "Let's go for a walk."' The teacher then reads the excerpt starting on page 84 with '"Lockie wants to try it on skis"' and ending on page 86 with 'And vomited on the first person he came to.'

10.1 The description of Vicki suggests she is expert at water-skiing. List three phrases that give this impression.

See the Appendix for guidelines on listening tasks before you attempt these questions and activities.

10.2 Decide whether the following statements are true or false.
  a Mr Streeton takes the credit for Vicki's performance on water-skis.
  b The parents at the picnic talk about anything but money and business.
  c 'They talked about cash-flow the way Lockie might talk about waves' means they know nothing about cash-flow.
  d The people at the picnic make Lockie feel uncomfortable.

10.3 Lockie agrees to ski probably because:
  a he doesn't want to seem a coward
  b he wants the chance to impress Vicki
  c he doesn't want to be laughed at by rich kids
  d all of the above.

10.4 Lockie finds water-skiing:
  a just possible
  b completely impossible
  c amazingly easy
  d great fun.

10.5 The phrase 'went round swinging like a rusty gate' means that Lockie's action was:
  a smooth
  b circular
  c jerky
  d gate-like.

10.6 Explain in your own words why Lockie is described as a human torpedo.

10.7 What makes this excerpt from the book entertaining? Make notes on the situation, the characters and the language before writing your answer.

POPULAR culture

chapter 2

In this chapter you will read, view and listen to texts that are related to popular culture and discuss and define the term 'popular culture'. A great deal of popular culture is generated by the media (including television, radio and film).

This chapter contains:
- an advertisement
- a song lyric
- reviews
- infotainment texts
- an interview
- magazine feature articles
- newspaper reports
- a novel excerpt.

You will have the opportunity to write:
- a creative piece
- a review
- an explanation
- a submission
- questions for your class members
- a 'twenty-five words or less' competition
- language analysis.

1. **IF MUSIC BE ...**
   Sony
   Elissa Blake
   'Various artists: Triple J Hottest 100 Vol. 5'
   Neil Finn (Crowded House)
   'Don't Dream It's Over'

2. **EVERYTHING OLD ...**
   Jeremy Vincent
   'Rebels without pause'
   Mark Juddery
   'A joyful, silly romp'

3. **HEROES AND IDOLS**
   Andrew Humphreys
   'Hot idol: Lucy Lawless'
   'Xenite hangouts'
   Keith Austin
   'Schlock, battle and spice'
   Nicole Triantafillou
   'A brave walk on the wildside'

4. **SPICE UP YOUR LIFE**
   Tom Moon
   'Help wanted: no talent needed'

5. **TITANIC GAMES**
   Linda Bruce
   'Disaster revisited'
   '20 fast facts: Leonardo DiCaprio'

6. **SPONSORSHIP**
   Adam Heimlich
   'The company they keep'

7. **YOUNG FILM-MAKERS**
   Richard Jinman
   'Teens turn the corner to film the nitty gritty'

8. Listening
   ROCK'N'ROLL
   Peter Goldsworthy
   Maestro

1 if MUSIC be...

advertisement

Sony

What is popular culture? Generally when we use the term 'our culture' we are referring to all the facets of our lifestyle that have been built up over the generations. Our culture includes our language, belief systems, religion, music, books, clothing, television, film, theatre, habits and sport. In fact it includes everything about the way we are.

BETWEEN THE LINES

1.1 So, what is 'popular culture'? In groups, discuss the term and write a definition. Compare definitions around the class.

1.2 Who is the intended audience of the Sony advertisement?

1.3 The visual impact of the advertisement depends on:
   a colloquial language
   b exaggeration
   c a simple statement
   d ignorance.

> **1.3** Refer to the Appendix for guidelines on analysing visual texts.
>
> **1.3** A definition of 'colloquial language' appears in the Key Terms section of the Appendix.

1.4 The message of the advertisement is:
   a you should not kick a Sony Walkman
   b Sony tapes produce the best sound quality in Sony Walkmans
   c other tapes produce bad sound quality in Sony Walkmans
   d other tapes do not fit into Sony Walkmans.

1.5 The language of the advertisement is:
   a effective because there's not much to read
   b difficult because it is technical and detailed
   c effective because it is simple and direct
   d not effective because it is in small print.

Elissa Blake
'Various artists: Triple J Hottest 100 Vol. 5'

For many young people, music is popular culture.

review

BETWEEN THE LINES

Read the review on page 28 and then complete the following questions and activities.

1.6 This CD is described as 'another snapshot of the nation's musical taste' (line 1) and 'a time capsule' (line 5). Lines 1–5 indicate that the CD:
   a features music popular with Australians in 1997
   b features music popular with Australians of all ages
   c features music popular with Triple J listeners in 1997
   d represents only one view of popular music.

1.7 'The concept is simple' (line 3) means the:
   a idea is simplistic
   b procedure is easy
   c idea is simple
   d theory is simple.

> **1.7** Check the difference in meaning between 'simplistic' and 'simple'. Have your dictionary on hand at all times.

1.8 The language of the review is:
  a relaxed and conversational
  b detailed and difficult to follow
  c humorous and colloquial
  d sophisticated and formal.

1.9 Write five or six lines giving evidence to support the answer you chose in 1.8.

1.10 Elissa Blake has written a review that is:
  a biased
  b balanced
  c complicated
  d uninformative.

1.11 Write eight or ten lines giving evidence to support the answer you chose in 1.10.

1.12 Identify two particular features of this collection that Blake highlights in the review.

Various Artists
Triple J Hottest 100 Vol. 5
VIRGIN

Another snapshot of the nation's musical taste from the folks at Triple J.

The concept is simple. Ask the listeners of Triple J to vote for their favourite songs of 1997, chuck them in order from one to 100, shave off the excess and release a time capsule double CD. Hours of listening from the Verve's classic single 'Bitter Sweet Symphony' to irritating one hit wonders such as Blue Boy's 'Remember Me'. This year the Australian contingent is the strongest yet. The Whitlams took the number one spot with 'No Aphrodisiac' followed by Jebediah's 'Leaving Home' (number 11), silverchair's 'Freak' (13), the Superjesus' 'Down Again' (14), Living End's 'Prisoner of Society' (15), Cordrazine's 'Crazy' (17), Nick Cave's 'Into My Arms' (18) and Regurgitator's 'Everyday Formula' (19). Other Australian acts include diana ah naid, Spiderbait, Grinspoon, the Mavis's, Front End Loader and Kylie Minogue. The collection reveals 1997 was a year of strong pop singles from 'One Angry Dwarf and 200 Solemn Faces' by Ben Fold's Five, 'Walkin' On the Sun' by Smash Mouth, 'Brimful of Asha' by Cornershop and 'Monkey Wrench' by the Foo Fighters. Even if you are already sick of some of these songs, this collection will be a treat in five or six years time.

★★★

Elissa Blake
Rolling Stone, October 1998

Neil Finn (Crowded House)
'Don't Dream It's Over'

song lyric

It is alleged that when Paul McCartney of The Beatles heard this song he said that Neil Finn was the greatest songwriter of the twentieth century.

> There is freedom within, there is freedom without
> Try to catch the deluge in a paper cup
> There's a battle ahead, many battles are lost
> But you'll never see the end of the road
> While you're travelling with me
>
> *Chorus*
> *Hey now, hey now*
> *Don't dream it's over*
> *Hey now, hey now*
> *When the world comes in*
> *They come, they come*
> *To build a wall between us*
> *We know they won't win*
>
> Now I'm towing my car, there's a hole in the roof
> My possessions are causing me suspicion but there's no proof
> In the paper today tales of war and of waste
> But you turn right over to the TV page
>
> *Repeat Chorus*
>
> Now I'm walking again to the beat of a drum
> And I'm counting the steps to the door of your heart
> Only the shadows ahead barely clearing the roof
> Get to know the feeling of liberation and relief
>
> *Hey now, hey now*
> *Don't dream it's over*
> *Hey now, hey now*
> *When the world comes in*
> *They come, they come*
> *To build a wall between us*
> *Don't ever let them win*

BETWEEN THE LINES

1.13 In groups, discuss the main idea of each stanza and of the chorus. In your own words, write down what you think the song is about.

1.14 Writing
Listen to the song in class and, in your own words, write down words and phrases that describe the feelings expressed by the song.
Develop your list into a piece of creative writing. Try to write about 300 words.

2 everything OLD...

review **Jeremy Vincent**
'Rebels without pause'

Everything old is new again. During 1998, the 1970s hit film *Grease* was re-released, sparking interest in the stage show.

MUSICAL THEATRE GREASE

Rebels without pause

The Arena Production, Melbourne Park

Grease lightning: Dannii Minogue, Craig McLachlan and an energetic cast pack quite a performance

1 Producer John Frost has another hit on his hands. In the world of entertainment, bigger isn't always better, but this spacious, spectacular arena production of *Grease* really works, with a generosity of spirit that overflows to the thousands of adoring fans who come to watch it.

2 Lively, energy-packed performers bounce around the stage, singing and dancing their hearts out.

3 They are the pupils of Rydell High and, whether you like it or not, these boys and girls are going to have a good time. And the audience laps it up.

4 Inspired more by the film starring Olivia Newton-John and John Travolta than the original Broadway musical, this production is staged on Brian Thomson's stylised record-player set, its LP a multi-faceted revolve that rises and falls to create all manner of locations in and around Rydell. Music director Paul White and his team sit in a flying saucer high above the stage. After failing to perform on opening night, when patrons were treated to a semi-concert version, the set still caused a few heart-stopping moments towards the end of the second evening performance. Technology is a marvellous thing, but, for better or worse, it often has a talent to upstage. However, apart from the jukebox finale hiccup, in this show the slick performers are the stars.

5 As Danny Zuko, former Neighbour Craig McLachlan has the audience in the palm of his extremely talented hand. There was more than a touch of *Rocky Horror* showmanship in this unique portrayal of the lovestruck school tough. Yet McLachlan struts with such confidence and panache that you instantly fall for the antics. Beyond Zuko's fey characteristics when confronted with his

summer sweetheart, McLachlan swaggers his way to the top of the class with his vocals and even a solo guitar spot.

6   Jane Scali's Sandy has just the right amount of saccharine to tip the balance in the female dormitory, where virginal attitudes aren't meant to last. Her performance matures beautifully into the sexpot that inspires 'You're the One That I Want' and it remains a mystery why her billing is not up there with the other stars.

7   Scali's talent certainly towers over that of Dannii Minogue, who turns the key role of Rizzo into a staccato-gesturing, two-dimensional strutter, totally missing a golden character opportunity. Her singing is often flat. From among the key support groups, the Pink Ladies and the T Bars, there otherwise emerges a splendid roll call of talent, performances that create totally engaging characters, many with show-stopping solos. Anthony Warlow's flying 'Teen Angel' is a suitably camped up showpiece, singing like a dream, dressed in white leather and chewing aggressively on gum. Doug Parkinson and Glen Shorrock make cameo appearances as Vince Fontaine and Johnny Casino, respectively, while Totti Goldsmith is an unnecessary luxury in the grossly reduced role of Miss Lynch.

8   Trudy Dalgleish's lighting and Angus Strathie's costumes (aside from Sandy's plastic-look transformation suit) are impressive in their subtlety, while David Gilmore's direction for the most part uses the space wisely and, with the help of segue music, his show moves forward well.

9   Exceptions are an under-use of the revolve, especially in Sandy's solo ballad, 'Hopelessly Devoted To You' and elsewhere as a means to create a more effective in-the-round dialogue delivery.

10   At times, too, the step-ups on the revolve appeared uncomfortably high. Ross Coleman's choreography often owes more to *Saturday Night Fever* than to *Rock Around the Clock*, but his boyish male ensemble (most are vertically challenged and appear straight out of primary school) move unquestionably well. *Grease* IS the word. Go see it.

Australian, 27 April 1998

BETWEEN THE LINES

2.1 'Rebels without pause' (headline) and 'grease lightning' (photo caption) are examples of:
   a puns
   b metaphors
   c similes
   d personification.

> **2.1** Definitions of 'metaphor', 'pun', 'personification' and 'simile' appear in the Key Terms section of the Appendix.

2.2 Explain the reasons for the answer you chose in 2.1.

2.3 Does the photo help to convey the opinion of the reviewer? Why or why not?

2.4 The second sentence in paragraph 1 implies that the:
   a size of the production is part of its success
   b size of the production does not matter
   c show is a success because it is spectacular
   d fans adore it regardless of entertainment value.

2.5 Describe the stage design (paragraph 4) in your own words.

2.6 'Technology is a marvellous thing, but, for better or worse, it often has a talent to upstage' (paragraph 4). Explain this sentence and the figure of speech being used by the writer.

> **2.6** A definition of 'figure of speech' appears in the Key Terms section of the Appendix.

2.7 In the sentence 'Beyond Zuko's fey characteristics when confronted with his summer sweetheart...' (paragraph 5), the word 'fey' means:
a dying
b spellbound
c eccentric
d tough.

2.8 'Dannii Minogue... turns the key role of Rizzo into a staccato-gesturing, two-dimensional strutter' (paragraph 7). Explain this description in your own words.

2.9 This review comments on each of the following aspects of the show:
- the performance of the lead actors
- the lighting and costumes
- the direction of the show
- the performance of the supporting cast
- the general impact of the production
- a description of the set and its operation
- the name of the producer
- the name of the director
- the names of other stage personnel.

Identify each of these in the review and note the order in which they occur.

2.10 Writing

Using the review of *Grease* as a model, write a review of a play, musical or concert that you have attended or viewed on television. Write about 300–400 words.

review

Mark Juddery
'A joyful, silly romp'

The re-release of the movie *Grease* was a surprising success and shows that what was popular when your parents were young is not necessarily 'old hat'.

BETWEEN THE LINES

Read the review on page 33 and then complete the following questions and activities.

2.11 The headline of the review indicates that the reviewer thinks *Grease*:
a is a childish movie
b has some value
c is a waste of time
d is just for fun.

2.12 'To look back nostalgically' (paragraph 1) means to:
  a long for the past
  b idealise the past
  c suffer from homesickness
  d return home mentally.

2.13 The second paragraph suggests that:
  a *Singin' in the Rain* was made in the 1920s
  b the 1950s weren't much fun
  c we prefer the past
  d we live in the past.

2.14 The word 'emulated' (paragraph 3) means:
  a criticised
  b competed with
  c imitated
  d surpassed.

2.15 Research the meanings of 'golden age' and 'classics' (paragraph 5).

2.16 The songs are aided by 'polished choreography' (paragraph 5). This means:
  a flawless dance routines
  b dancing on polished floors
  c excellent design
  d polished performance.

2.17 Rewrite paragraph 8 in your own words.

2.18 What is the 'denouement' (paragraph 9) of a story? Explain why you think the reviewer is disappointed by the denouement of this story.

> **2.18** A definition of 'denouement' appears in the Narrative Structure section of the Appendix.

A joyful, silly romp

Cinema

By MARK JUDDERY

Grease (PG). At Greater Union Manuka, Hoyts Belconnen, Pacific Cinemas Tuggeranong and Cosmopolitan Twin Cinemas Woden.

★★★★½

1 With the twentieth anniversary re-issue of *Grease*, complete with digital soundtrack, we have another chance to look back nostalgically on a 1978 film which looked back nostalgically on the '50s.

2 This actually makes some kind of sense. After all, I doubt that the real '50s were ever as much fun as in *Grease*. The best movie musical of that decade (or any decade), *Singin' in the Rain*, was set in the late '20s, with several songs from the era. Proof that, whenever you live, the past is always more fun.

3 Despite the hype, *Grease* falls short of being 'the greatest movie musical of all time' (by my own calculations, it comes about seventeenth), but it is probably the only rock'n'roll

film that ever emulated the innocent fun of the golden age of Hollywood musicals.

4 The smooth Danny (John Travolta) could have been played by Gene Kelly in another era. Debbie Reynolds or, well, Sandra Dee could easily have played his love, Olivia Newton-John's wholesome Sandy.

5 Like the classics from the golden age, it has some catchy, instantly likeable songs and agreeable chorus numbers, aided by polished choreography. The musical numbers, which once seemed like innocent fun, now come across as witty, affectionate and at times hilarious parodies of both the '50s and the musical genre.

6 One exception is the famous duet 'You're the One That I Want'. Pandering to the disco generation, it was a huge hit in its time, but it is now the most dated song of the film. Unlike the other tunes, which fit snugly into the fantasy period setting, it sounds exactly like a remnant of the '70s.

7 It is a joyful romp, full of silly stereotypes. Though they were too old to play high-schoolers, the energy of the cast is still contagious.

8 Much has been said about Travolta and Newton-John, but Stockard Channing was equally good (even musically) as the more three-dimensional Rizzo, laboured with the film's few serious moments.

9 The story, empty and enjoyable, is let down by its denouement. Its message: to find true love, don't be yourself.

10 True, it's all part of the fantasy, but it's something of a cop-out. One small downer in a near-classic flick.

★ Of little merit.
★★ Not a total waste of time and money, but not great value.
★★★ Value for money without being great cinema.
★★★★ A sound investment.
★★★★★ Full value in every sense

Canberra Times, 4 July 1998

3 heroes and IDOLS

magazine feature article

Andrew Humphreys
'Hot idol: Lucy Lawless'

Tele... heroes and idols.

BETWEEN THE LINES

Read the magazine feature article on page 35 and then complete the following questions and activities.

3.1 Research the Titans (paragraph 1).

3.2 The word closest in meaning to 'carnage' (paragraph 1) is:
  a massacre
  b revenge
  c result
  d homicide.

3.3 Divide the following terms between groups in the class and develop definitions for them: 'syndicated television', 'savvy cult filmmakers', 'smart TV pretending that it's not', 'heavy on the cheese', 'dark, surreal drama', 'full-tilt slapstick', 'classic Hollywood comedy' and 'Hong Kong action avant garde'.

3.4 Which features of this article create a conversational tone? Write eight to ten lines.

> **3.4** A definition of 'tone' appears in the Key Terms section of the Appendix.

Hot Idol Lucy Lawless

1 Trouble with a vengeful God? Titans destroying your village? Want to see hot justice summarily dispensed by a sword-wielding babe in a leather mini with a blood-curdling battle cry and a see-you-in-hell steely glare? Easy—call Xena, Warrior Princess. Stand back and watch the carnage.

2 Millions of people in over sixty countries do just that every week, making 'Xena: Warrior Princess' a spin-off from the equally, successful 'Hercules: The Legendary Journeys' now in its fourth season, one of the biggest syndicated television shows in the world. Bigger than 'Baywatch'. Bigger than any of the 'Star Trek' spin-offs. And 'Xena' is good. Produced by savvy cult filmmakers Sam Raimi and Rob Tapert, creators of 'The Evil Dead', 'Army of Darkness' and 'Darkman', 'Xena' is smart TV pretending that it's not. Heavy on the cheese, 'Xena: Warrior Princess' ranges from dark, surreal drama to full-tilt slapstick, often within the same episode. It's influenced as much by classic Hollywood comedy as by the Hong Kong action avant garde. Standing tall in the middle of it all is Xena herself, a woman with a troubled past and blood (lots of it) on her hands doing her best to be a good person in a not-so-good world.

3 Xena is a hero, an idol. And Lucy Lawless, the thirty-year-old New Zealand actor who plays her, is now a star.

Rolling Stone, October 1998

'Xenite hangouts'

Lucy Lawless's character, Xena, has an enthusiastic following, so it is not surprising that several websites about her have been created.

> **infotainment**

BETWEEN THE LINES

Read the infotainment text on page 36 and then complete the following questions and activities.

3.5 Imagine that you need to explain the information in this text to someone who has never watched an episode of 'Xena' and who does not understand the World Wide Web. In your groups, work out a simple explanation of the World Wide Web and web addresses and simplify the information given about 'Xena'. You will need to research the meanings of words such as 'quasi-academic' and 'chakram'.

> **3.5** Refer to the Appendix for guidelines on writing explanation texts.

3.6 If someone had never watched an episode of 'Xena', what impression would the photograph give of the television show? Analyse the photograph carefully before writing your answer. Write about a page.

> **3.6** Refer to the Appendix for guidelines on analysing visual texts.

Xenite Hangouts

1 *Xena Online Resources*:
http://www.xenite.org/xenaonln.htm
An excellent starting point for the budding Xenite.

Tom's Xena Site: http://www.xenafan.com
5 The first 'fan page' on the web. Lotsa games and other fun.

Whoosh!: http://www.whoosh.org
Hanker for some 'quasi-academic, quasi-intellectual' Xena fun? Then take a peek at *Whoosh!* (it's
10 the sound Xena's chakram makes as it flies through the air), the online journal of the International Association of Xena Studies. It specialises in essays, commentaries and analysis of all things Xena. From the light-hearted to the
15 not so light-hearted, essays on the site include 'The Evolution of the Sidekick', 'Law and Economics in "Xena: Warrior Princes"', 'The Shock of Recognition: A Lesbian Appreciation of "Xena: Warrior Princess"' and 'Tall, Dark and Deadly: A
20 Comparative Look at Xena and Emma Peel'

Lawless in action as Xena.

Rolling Stone, 7 October 1998

---

review

Keith Austin
'Schlock, battle and spice'

'Hercules' and 'Xena' are television shows that demonstrate that popular culture can appeal to all age groups.

BETWEEN THE LINES

Read the review on page 37 and then complete the following questions and activities.

3.7 Keith Austin believes 'the "Greeks" get it every time' (paragraph 2) because:
   a those who demand respect are preferred
   b tough Greek heroes are more fun
   c the viewers are tired of cuddly Daryl
   d Greek shows are more entertaining.

3.8 Both shows 'have their tongue planted firmly in their cheek' (paragraph 3) means:
   a the shows will only appeal to younger audiences
   b in both shows the actors can't speak properly
   c fighters have their tongues in their cheeks while fighting
   d the scripts are deliberately funny while appearing serious.

Schlock, battle and spice

Hercules and Xena
Ten, 6.30 p.m. and 7.30 p.m.

1. Take two hours of prime-time television and fill it with a schlocky mix of gratuitous violence, sweaty biceps, buns of steel, thighs of hammered titanium, lesbian undertones and male bonding—hey, hey, it's Saturday again!
2. And when it comes to a choice between cuddly Daryl or the redoubtable Hercules and the steely Xena, the 'Greeks' get it every time.
3. There are some similarities between the two shows—both have their tongue planted firmly in their cheek, both work for adults and children alike and both feature truly awful sets.
4. Mind you, any adult who watches any of these shows alone needs to see a shrink. Those of us with kids will already know that they are compulsory viewing. If you don't have a kid, borrow one.
5. This week, sadly, the 'Hercules' offering is a multiple repeat, and a two-part repeat at that.
6. To be fair, every episode is a repeat, given that Hercules is continually called to save some crumbling collection of hayseed homes and shops from the local gorgon/dragon/warlord.
7. Something goes wrong and the crumbling hayseed denizens of the aforesaid village are revealed as smelly ingrates, until big Herc triumphs over evil and spreads the peace and love message.
8. It's a morality tale with oomph. Alright, so the big man solves most of his problems by punching someone's lights out, but it's always in a noble cause (maybe they should have sent Kevin Sorbo into Kuwait).
9. Tonight, Herc goes in search of Fire, which Hera has stolen from poor old Prometheus, with Anthony Quinn twinkling as Zeus.
10. Which brings us to Xena, the bionic babe of the '90s, a Spice Woman if I ever saw one.
11. Lucy Lawless's great talent is keeping a straight face while uttering such immortal lines as: 'It's a dark, wicked thing that must be destroyed.'
12. Tonight's dark, wicked thing is Gabrielle's baby—yes, you read it correctly—and an immaculate conception at that, on what seems to be a walking tour of Britain, during which they encounter The Evil One, some flying banshees and the original knights of a round table.
13. The writers even manage to squeeze in the sword in the stone. It waits in the polystyrene castle for the future king to free Britain from the invaders' yoke.
14. You can see it coming a mile off, but when Xena strolled past and pulled the sword out ('nice blade') I laughed my socks off at the sheer lunacy of it all.

Sydney Morning Herald, 22–28 June 1998

Awaiting Xena tonight...Gabrielle (Rene O'Connor).

3.9 'Every episode is a repeat' (paragraph 6) means:
 a the television channel keeps repeating the series
 b every episode has the same plot
 c Hercules has to save the same village every time
 d Hercules always punches someone.

3.10 Definitions of 'cliché', 'metaphor' and 'pun' appear in the Key Terms section of the Appendix.	**3.10** Lucy Lawless has to keep a straight face (paragraph 11) because the line she has to say is: **a** a pun **b** a cliché **c** a metaphor **d** serious.
	3.11 Austin's comments about 'Xena' suggest that he: **a** enjoys the show because it is so unrealistic it is funny **b** dislikes the show because he thinks it is schlocky **c** enjoys the show because he likes the actor **d** dislikes the show because it is tongue-in-cheek humour.
3.12 Refer to the Appendix for guidelines on analysing visual texts.	**3.12** Study the photographs on pages 36 and 37. Comment on the contrasts between the two female characters.
3.13 Refer to the Appendix for guidelines on sentence types. Definitions of 'rhetorical questions' and 'tone' appear in the Key Terms section of the Appendix.	**3.13** Study the language used in the three texts about 'Xena' and make a list of the features that are similar and those that are different. Before you write your list make notes on the vocabulary used, the types of sentences used, the use of questions and the writer's tone.

interview

Nicole Triantafillou
'A brave walk on the wildside'

Realism is also a feature of current popular culture. In 1998 and 1999 the ABC screened the drama 'Wildside'. It is set in Sydney's Kings Cross and exposes the more sinister side of city life.

BETWEEN THE LINES

Read the interview on page 39 and then complete the following questions and activities.

3.14 Decide whether the following statements are true or false.
   a The series is described as 'brave TV' (paragraph 4) because it deals realistically with the ugly and dangerous aspects of life.
   b 'You can start off with plan A but you'll end up with plan M' (paragraph 5). This refers to usual Australian drama.
   c Aaron Pederson's work experience shows that he is likely to go wherever the moment takes him.
   d Aaron Pederson considers his work is important for aboriginal kids.

3.15 Explain in your own words what Aaron Pederson means by the statement: 'aboriginal actors are actors not aboriginal people acting' (paragraph 12).

3.16 Refer to the Appendix for guidelines on analysing visual texts.

3.16 Comment on the camera angle used to photograph Aaron Pederson and the impression the photograph gives you of Aaron's personality.

A brave walk on the wildside

1. Nicole Triantafillou talks to Aaron Pederson on why gritty drama 'Wildside' is challenging Australian audiences

2. '"Wildside" suits me to a "t,"' says Aaron Pederson, who plays Wildside lawyer, Vince Cellini. 'It suits my headspace and suits me as a performer.'

3. The show has made both critics and viewers sit up and watch with its gritty and realistic exposé of street life in Sydney's Kings Cross. 'Wildside' isn't afraid to take a snapshot view of the darker, uglier underbelly of city life and feed its audience an unsanitised version of it. Even the good guys are flawed.

4. 'It's not like anything Australian audiences are used to seeing in local drama, it's very brave TV,' says Aaron who's particularly proud of being involved in such a ground breaking show.

5. 'I've always had some problems with the way Australian drama has been dealt with in the past. Just the way that it's always so contrived. Life's not like that. You can start off with plan A, but you'll end up with plan M. The beautiful thing with acting on this show is that we create a moment but we just don't know what's going to happen in the end.'

6. Aaron isn't surprised at the fuss the show has so far generated. He says that it's time Australian television progressed to the next stage. And it's a leap made easier when a show boasts acting talents like Tony Martin ('E Street', 'Heartbreak High'), Rachael Blake, John Howard and Paul Pantano, the actor Aaron calls the 'young Brando'.

> 'I want to be involved in pioneering the idea that aboriginal actors are actors, not aboriginal people acting.'

7. 'Young Paul is magical to work with. We all do a lot of improvisation, but Paul is a raver, he never shuts up. Sometimes I've just got to tell him to shut up and let me do my lines! But he improvises and throws the moment of reality right at you.'

8. Choosing to go wherever the moment of reality takes him is something Aaron seems always prepared for. He's worked as a producer, director and presenter for the ABC show 'Blackout', starred with Bryan Brown in the film *Dead Heart*, co-hosted 'Gladiators' on Channel Seven and was Cleo's Bachelor of the Year in 1994.

9. 'It's not the Nobel peace prize but at least it gives aboriginal kids a chance to say, "well, maybe I can achieve things too".'

10. To get a grip on the role of Vince, he spent a week observing high profile solicitor, Chris Murphy.

11. 'Chris is interesting, he's a flamboyant, strong-headed character, and he's a very hard worker. Lawyers often have twelve cases to work on at the same time. I got an idea of the corporate aspect of law. The world of Kings Cross is obviously very different.'

12. It's also a very different world for indigenous actors like Aaron who are breaking the stereotypes. 'I want to be involved in pioneering the idea that aboriginal actors are actors not aboriginal people acting. My attitude is I'm from a privileged generation and I have nothing to lose. My motivation goes beyond me, it's got to do with my people and culture,' explains Aaron.

Soap World, 7 April 1998

4 SPICE up your life

newspaper report

Tom Moon
'Help wanted: no talent needed'

In May 1998, Geri Halliwell (Ginger Spice) left the Spice Girls. There was a good deal of discussion in the press about who would take her place.

BETWEEN THE LINES

Read the newspaper report on page 41 and then complete the following questions and activities.

4.1 What does the headline of the report signal about the writer's attitude to the Spice Girls?

4.2 Study the illustration used for this report, including the heading and the captions below each photograph. In groups, research the four singers pictured and explain why the writer has suggested that they might be called 'Low-Cal Spice', 'Old Spice', 'Scarier Spice' and 'Scariest Spice'. Write about ten to twelve lines.

4.3 Decide whether the following statements are true or false. The inclusion of the illustration suggests:
  a the Spice Girls have no talent compared with these singers
  b the writer has a sense of humour
  c these singers would like to join the Spice Girls
  d any singer could replace Ginger Spice
  e these singers are far too talented to be seriously considered as replacements.

4.4 Paragraph 4 suggests that:
  a the media could make a great deal of money
  b Ginger Spice could have a media career
  c the media is playing a game
  d the publicity could make money for the group.

4.5 What does the term 'Spice whirl' (paragraph 5) imply about a life with the Spice Girls?

4.6 Explain the meaning of paragraph 12 in your own words.

4.7 The 'star-making machine' (paragraph 14) refers to:
  a the public relations organisation behind the Spice Girls
  b the adulation of the fans, which creates the stars
  c the drive and determination of the new girl
  d clever lighting and staging at concerts.

Help wanted: no talent needed

By TOM MOON in Los Angeles

1 SO YOU wanna be a Spice Girl?

2 As you probably know, there's an opening.

3 Already, rumours are circulating that there will be a talent search for an American to replace Geri Halliwell, 25, the unofficial spokeswoman of the Spice Girls, who announced at the weekend she was departing to pursue a solo career.

4 If played correctly by these masters of media, the departure of Ginger Spice could blossom into another PR bonanza.

5 Soon, after the remaining Spice Girls finish their forty-city North American tour, some now-anonymous young woman could win a life in the Spice whirl.

6 That person would savour the glamour of being involved with last year's top-selling pop group, which has sold more than 30 million copies of its two albums, Spice and Spiceworld, worldwide.

7 What are the job requirements?

8 History offers a clue. When the British five-piece was created in 1996, its members were recruited through magazine ads that sought attractive women with street-smarts and drive.

9 'No singing or dancing experience necessary,' read the solicitation.

10 How prophetic. Even before they were famous, the Girls and since-fired manager Simon Fuller knew one crucial thing about celebrity in the waning minutes of the century: that talent is far less important than image.

WHO COULD FILL GINGER'S PLATFORM SHOES

CELINE DION: Low-Cal Spice

MADONNA: Old Spice

COURTNEY LOVE: Scarier Spice

MARILYN MANSON: Scariest Spice

11 The trick is to become a symbol, to develop a marketing niche.

12 Brandishing Girl Power like a talisman, they became a bubblegum phenomenon with a fiercely loyal core audience of girls between the ages of seven and fourteen.

13 Girls could be anything—and any way—they pleased, they counselled. And the first high-concept girl group demonstrated the message in many forms—one Spice was sporty, one sexy. There could be, they seemed to say, a different Spice for every mood.

14 Once they've got the new girl, the star-making machine will kick in again.

15 An accommodating cadre of songwriters will whip up a few thematic ditties—limiting themselves to four or five melody notes, so as not to tax those pipes. The myth-makers will work their magic.

16 And soon Halliwell will be a distant memory.

17 This is what it will take to be a Spice Girl: the willingness to be moulded, shaped and sold, not as a musician but as a prefab pop tart.

18 The ability to play a cardboard role. A high threshold for public humiliation. A desire to be pretty. And pretty blank.

19 One thing's for sure: this is one case where nobody can claim those oft-cited 'creative differences'.

Daily Telegraph, 3 June 1998

> **4.8** A definition of 'irony' appears in the Key Terms section of the Appendix.

> **4.9** A definition of 'pun' appears in the Key Terms section of the Appendix.

4.8 Identify and explain two examples of irony in the report.

4.9 Find two examples of puns in paragraphs 17 and 18, and explain them.

4.10 The message of the report is:
  a girls can do anything
  b creative differences don't matter
  c talent is far less important than image
  d the music needs to be simple.

5 titanic GAMES

review

Linda Bruce
'Disaster revisited'

When the unsinkable *Titanic* went to the bottom of the North Atlantic in 1912, a remarkable story was launched. The film *Titanic* is one of several about the disaster and it has furthered movie careers and launched CD-ROMs, games and CDs.

BETWEEN THE LINES

Read the review on page 43 and then complete the following questions and activities.

5.1 Explain what a CD-ROM is and the purpose of the 'requirements' section at the beginning of the review.

5.2 Research words and terms in the review with which you may not be familiar. Examples include 'death throes', 'blockbuster movie', 'ragtime tune' and 'stoker'.

5.3 Linda Bruce describes the CD-ROM as 'seductively educative' (paragraph 3) because it:
  a is a dramatic reconstruction
  b includes a lot of detail
  c teaches without appearing to
  d preserves the ambiguity of history.

5.4 'Attention to detail' (paragraph 3) is suggested as one of the features of *Titanic—An Interactive Journey*. What examples are given?

5.5 Research the reasons why 'social inequalities sealed the fates of the majority of third-class passengers' (paragraph 5).

(continued p. 44)

DISASTER REVISITED

You've seen the movie, but the truth about the *Titanic* is on this disc, says Linda Bruce.

CD-ROM OF THE WEEK

Titanic—
An Interactive Journey
★★★★½
Price: $49.95
Requirements: Windows 3.1x, 486/DX33 processor, 8Mb RAM, 10Mb hard disk space, 256 colours, 2x CD-ROM drive; Macintosh LCIII, System 7.01x, 6Mb RAM, 256 colours, 2x CD-ROM drive
Distributor: Europress

10 COPIES TO BE WON!
The distributor of *Titanic—An Interactive Journey*, has ten copies of the CD-ROM to give away. In twenty-five words or less, tell us why you would like to win a copy. Entries close Friday, 31 July. Winners will be published in the 15 August issue of *Living IT*.

1 On a starry night on 16 April 1912, the 'unsinkable' *Titanic* went down off the icy water of Newfoundland, taking 1250 men, women and children with her. We know now it simply did not have enough lifeboats. But during its death throes, just what did the band play?

2 *Nearer My God to Thee*, claims the blockbuster movie. But others argue this would only have fuelled the distress of the passengers that remained. The ragtime tune *Autumn* is considered the more likely candidate.

3 The appealing thing about *Titanic—An Interactive Journey*, is just how well it reproduces the drama of that star-filled night, while preserving the ambiguity of its history. As you traipse through the testimony of the survivors, both songs are referred to as the final musical backdrop. This attention to detail makes it compelling and seductively educative.

4 The conditions of the first-, second- and third-class passengers and the crew—particularly the wretched stokers—are detailed with period photos. A day-by-day diary reveals the ship's history, its opulence, and the terror and heroism triggered by the tragedy.

5 You can see reproductions of warnings of the iceberg's presences that *Titanic's* captain ignored, and read first-person accounts of rescue efforts by the crew, the confusion on both sides of the Atlantic as friends and families waited for news, and how social inequalities sealed the fates of the majority of third-class passengers.

6 The CD-ROM also offers 600 period photographs with 200 original illustrations and more than 200 photographs of objects recovered from the *Titanic* after more than seventy-five years. However, the strength of the disc lies with the polished and entertaining re-enactment of US senator William Smith's probe into why so many lives were lost.

7 For the price, it's hard to quibble with this disc. But strictly speaking there is nothing interactive about it. In some ways you could get the same value from a video. However, there is an undeniable atmosphere to *Titanic— An Interactive Journey* that is rare in CD-ROMs. I found myself wanting to learn more of the fate of third-class passengers, or dipping into the stylish way some first-class passengers chose to meet their death.

8 Either way, *Titanic—An Interactive Journey* is itself a first-class voyage.

Weekend Australian,
25–26 July 1998

5.6 Linda Bruce believes the best feature of the CD-ROM is:
   a the price of $49.95
   b its inquiry into the reasons for the disaster
   c the atmosphere it creates
   d the detail it includes.

5.7 Linda Bruce:
   a thinks the title is appropriate
   b doesn't enjoy the journey
   c thinks a video would be as good
   d says the title is inaccurate.

5.8 Beginning with the phrase 'the truth about the *Titanic*' (by-line), list all the evidence showing that Linda Bruce approves of this CD-ROM. Look for visual as well as verbal evidence.

5.9 Writing
'TEN COPIES TO BE WON!
In twenty-five words or less, tell us why you would like to win a copy.'
Enter the competition and select the ten best entries from your class.

---

infotainment

'20 fast facts: Leonardo DiCaprio'

Leonardo DiCaprio's role in *Titanic* and other movies has made him a star. He has been written about, photographed and adored. He appears regularly in popular magazines and has become part of current popular culture.

BETWEEN THE LINES

Read the infotainment text on pages 45 and 46 and then complete the following questions and activities.

5.10 Refer to the Appendix for guidelines on analysing visual texts.

5.10 Study '20 fast facts: Leonardo DiCaprio', and then write ten 'fast facts' about the text, each focusing on one of the points listed below.
   - Why are the facts 'fast'?
   - The use of the name 'The DiCapster' to refer to DiCaprio.
   - The purpose of language such as 'well … duh!', 'yuck' and 'yeah, right!'
   - The purpose of anecdotes (fast facts 4, 5 and 6).
   - Word choice.
   - The effect of the photograph.
   - The tone.
   - The meaning of fast fact 13.
   - The meaning of the last sentence: 'Talk about a babe-fest!'
   - The success (or not) of this concept, that is, an article written as a series of 'fast facts'.

20 FAST FACTS
LEONARDO DICAPRIO

You can hire him in *Marvin's Room* this month! You can own him in *Romeo and Juliet*! Who? Well ... duh! Here's the coolest facts on The DiCapster!

1 Leonardo Wilhelm DiCaprio was named after the famous painter Leonardo DaVinci. An unborn Leo gave his mum a first kick while she was admiring a DaVinci painting in Rome!

2 He was born in Los Angeles on 11 November 1974. His dad, George, is Italian and his mum, Irmalin, is German. Leo was an only child (though he now has a stepbrother named Adam) and his parents divorced within a year of his birth. Poor tyke!

3 Leo's mum used to be a legal secretary but now works as his manager. His dad produces comic books out of the garage at home. Leo says his folks were pretty cool. 'Whatever I did, it would be something they'd already done. My dad would welcome it if I got a nose ring!'

4 Most people cherish the memory of their first kiss, but not Leo—he says the girl injected about a pound of spit into his mouth! When he walked away poor Leo had to spit it all out. Yuck!

5 Leo admits to having been more interested in entertaining schoolmates than doing homework. 'I could never focus on things I didn't want to learn,' he says. 'I used to do breakdancing skits with my friend at lunchtime.' Bet the teachers at the Centre for Enriched Studies and John Marshall High School in LA were impressed with that!

6 Leo made his TV debut at the age of five on the kids show 'Romper Room'. He was a little uncontrollable and was unceremoniously booted from the set for playing up!

7 The best advice Leo ever received from his dad was just after he'd been rejected at a casting call when he was ten: 'Someday, Leonardo, it will happen for you. Remember these words—just relax.' Thanks, Dad!

8 While on the prowl for an agent, Leonardo was asked to lose his ethnic-sounding name and change his haircut. One suggested name change was Lenny Williams ... yeah, right!

9 Early on, Leo acted in over thirty obscure ads and educational films, such as *How to Deal With a Parent Who Takes Drugs* and *Mickey's Safety Club*. He also did guest spots on TV shows like 'Lassie', 'The Outsiders', 'Roseanne' and 'Parenthood'.

Leo does his best 'I'm very mad' impersonation!

10 Leo's first movie role was in 1991's *Critters III*. It's the one role in his career that he refers to as 'embarrassing'.

11 Leo's first leading role was in *This Boy's Life* ... and while the movie didn't have box-office receipts rolling in, he did receive a few prestigious awards!

12 Leo prefers darker, more challenging roles to glitzy, glamorous ones. That's why he turned down the role of Robin in *Batman Forever*. 'I want to take my time with each role—that's how you plan a long career rather than doing it all at once in a big explosion,' he says. Right on!

13 Leo reckons the best thing about acting is getting lost in a character and actually getting paid for it! 'It's a great outlet to be a character but I'm not sure who I am. It seems that I change every day.'

14 One of Leo's greatest triumphs is the cool *What's Eating Gilbert Grape?* For this flick, Leo scored Academy Award and Golden Globe nominations!

15 The DiCapster also took home the Best Actor award at the 47th International Berlin Film Festival for *Romeo and Juliet*. Yey!

16 Leo is a massive car fanatic and owns three: a 1969 Mustang Convertible; a blue Jeep Grand Cherokee; and a BMW Coupe. You can bet the traffic authorities love him just as much as we do!

17 Leo is regularly seen at big Hollywood bashes with Johnny Depp, Liv Tyler and Courtney Love ... like the one thrown for Edward *Primal Fear* Norton's twenty-eighth birthday recently.

18 Of course, Leo's a real-life Romeo too! He's been linked to many beautiful women including Alicia Silverstone, Liv Tyler and Gwyneth Paltrow. Last reports were that he was dating model Kristin Zang.

19 Leo has an interesting way of keeping himself grounded—he likes hanging out with sweet people. 'I can't stand badasses. There's too many of them, especially my age, in LA.'

20 After *Titanic* and *The Man In the Iron Mask*, Leo is now filming the next Woody Allen film with Winona Ryder and Drew Barrymore. Talk about a babe-fest!

TV Hits, issue 112

6 SPONSORSHIP

magazine feature article

Adam Heimlich
'The company they keep'

This article raises the issue of the purpose of sponsorship and its role in creating popular culture icons.

BETWEEN THE LINES

Read the magazine feature article on page 47 and then complete the following questions and activities.

6.1 What is corporate sponsorship?

6.2 Explain the possible meanings of the headline 'The company they keep'. Give reasons for your answer.

6.3 A definition of 'pun' appears in the Key Terms section of the Appendix.

6.3 Explain the pun on 'sense' in 'dollars and sense' (subheading).

6.4 Adam Heimlich asks two questions in the introduction to his article. Identify each question and decide whether or not clear answers are provided by the information in the article. Write about ten or twelve lines on each question.

6.5 Which company do you think has the cleverest slogan? Give reasons for your answer.

6.6 A definition of 'irony' appears in the Key Terms section of the Appendix.

6.6 Identify two examples of irony in the article and explain the message that each provides.

6.7 Ericsson's Daryl Toor says of Celine Dion, 'Her demographic matches ours ideally, and she's noncontroversial.' What does this mean? Explain in your own words.

THE COMPANY THEY KEEP

The dollars and sense of corporate sponsorship.

The way Jay Coleman sees it, 'Concerts offer three revenue streams: ticket sales, merchandise and sponsorship.' He should know; until he came along, there were only two. His company, Entertainment Marketing Communications International, brokered the Rolling Stones' 1981 tour-sponsorship deal with Jovan. Sponsorship in rock & roll is now commonplace. Many artists and promoters say they couldn't tour without advertiser sponsorship—but do other benefits trickle down to the fans, or are these deals merely making big-ticket artists that much richer? **Adam Heimlich**

ACT	COMPANY	SLOGAN	THE COMPANY GETS	THE ARTIST GETS	THE CONSUMER GETS
ELTON JOHN	Citibank	Who says a bank can't rock & roll?	John to appear in Citibank's global ad campaign; he also did two private concerts for bank employees.	$5 million, according to the *Wall Street Journal*.	'Bennie and the Jets' ad nauseam.
MASSIVE ATTACK	Levi's	'It's not about slogans,' says Levi's Joe Townsend. 'It's about showing people we're supporting new music.'	The right to display banners at concerts and use Massive Attack music for a Japanese TV ad.	Low-key support for a worldwide tour.	The chance to see original triphoppers Massive Attack all around the world.
LILITH FAIR (Sarah McLachlan, Liz Phair, Missy Elliott, Sinéad O'Connor, Natalie Merchant, Queen Latifah, et al.)	Bioré (other sponsors include Levi's, Starbucks and Volkswagen)	Clean. Honest.	To give samples to its target audience. Bioré distributed 1.2 million cleansing strips in 1997 and is promoting spinoff products this year.	Tour support in the half-million-dollar range. Bioré, like all of Lilith's sponsors, will donate close to $100 000 to women's charities.	No blackheads and the reasonable ticket price of US$40.
CELINE DION	Ericsson mobile phones	The Power of Voice	Use of Dion's name, likeness and songs. Ericsson's Daryl Toor says, 'Her demographic matches ours ideally, and she's noncontroversial.'	Dion has said, 'Ericsson represents core values that are important to me.' One of which is an undisclosed amount in tour support.	To watch Dion performing in-the-round, with a state-of-the-art closed-circuit video system.
PLASTILINA MOSH (Mexican hip hop duo on Capital Records)	Apple Computers, Mexico	Think Different.	Branding on tour ads and the right to display its logo at shows and press conferences.	Two G3 Power Books, used to sequence samples during live shows, and a G3 desktop for their studio. Apple kicks in for tour ads.	Plastilina Mosh. Ricardo Shahin of Apple Mexico: 'They cannot imagine making music with computers different than Macintosh.'
SHANIA TWAIN	Gitano Jeanswear	Git Gitano Jeanswear.	To use Twain in promotional material, plus, when she wears denim onstage, it's Gitano.	An estimated $2 million for her first national concert tour, including local tour ads.	Reasonable ticket prices (US$25 to $30).
BLINK 1982	Billabong	None	Product visibility in the band's videos and press photos, but there's no contractual agreement.	Free Billabong clothing, accessories and wet suits, plus access to the half-pipe at Billabong's warehouse.	Extremely colourful videos.

Rolling Stone, October 1998

7 YOUNG film-makers

newspaper report

Richard Jinman
'Teens turn the corner to film the nitty gritty'

Young people themselves are an integral part of popular culture and now there are more opportunities for them to not only experience it as a consumer, but to create it.

Teens turn the corner to film the nitty gritty

1 Forget the Spice Girls and Leonardo DiCaprio. The teenagers competing in the ABC's 'Race Around the Corner' are more interested in public toilets, urinal etiquette, bad food, homesickness and baiting feminists.

2 Eight two-member teams from across Australia wrapped up a two-week ABC training course in Sydney yesterday with a screening of their graduation films. Six teams will be chosen to compete in the junior version of the ABC's 'Race Around the World', which begins on 3 August.

3 'Corner' teams will shoot six four-minute documentaries in their local area over a twelve week period. The ABC will air the series in a 5.30 p.m. timeslot from 28 September.

4 Travis Geldard and Nick Henderson, fifteen-year-old mates from Springwood, in the Blue Mountains, unleashed *Up Against the Wall*, a hilarious examination of male public urinal etiquette.

5 Ballarat's Tom Curtis and Bryce Ives, both fourteen, pushed the envelope even further with *Feminism: Is it Absolutely, Positively Necessary?*

6 Mike Munro-style, they burst into their local feminist bookstore … 'to drop some male macho comments and get the feminists real psyched up.'

7 Sadly, the store owner turned out to be '*so nice*' but Tom and Bryce haven't been dissuaded. In their coming films, vegetarians tour an abattoir and Victorian Premier Jeff Kennett becomes a teenager.

8 'We're just in it for fun,' said Ives. 'We want to get Jeff on a skateboard, slick his hair back—or chop it off.'

Double-teaming … young film-makers Nick Henderson, Shona Devlin, Katherine Venier and Travis Geldard yesterday.

9 Best friends Katherine Venier and Shona Devlin, both fifteen, were inspired by the quality of the food at their Sydney college. Their film *Overcoming Pond-Scum* was the result of the girls seeking cooking lessons at a local café as an antidote to their alma mater's canteen.

10 Katherine said a flow of good ideas was the key to the race.

11 'Something like body piercing can sound really good, but what do you do with it?' she said. 'Going deeper into stories is the hardest thing.'

Sydney Morning Herald
18 July 1998

BETWEEN THE LINES

7.1 The term 'nitty gritty' (headline) means:
   a nitpicking topics
   b sordid subjects
   c the core substance
   d unsavoury content.

7.2 Judging by the examples mentioned in the report, the focus of the documentaries depends on:
   a comparison and contrast
   b insulting people
   c revolting topics
   d good-humoured satire.

7.3 Study and discuss the composition of the photograph and the angle at which it was taken. Write about eight lines explaining the impact of this photograph on the story.

> **7.3** Refer to the Appendix for guidelines on analysing visual texts.

7.4 Writing
In groups, choose one of the topics mentioned in the report, or make up your own. Write a submission to the ABC, outlining how you would film a short documentary on your topic. Write about 300 to 400 words.

listening

8 rock'n'ROLL

novel excerpt

Peter Goldsworthy
Maestro

Many young people dream about forming their own band. After all, silverchair and Grinspoon did it.

BETWEEN THE LINES

Maestro, by Peter Goldsworthy, is set in Darwin and follows the experiences of Paul Crabbe as he grows up during the late 1960s. He is a talented

> Your teacher will read the synopsis and excerpt.

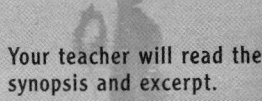

> See the Appendix for guidelines on listening tasks before you attempt these questions and activities.

pianist and has regular piano lessons with a famous 'maestro'. In his teenage years, he forms a rock'n'roll group with his friends and they plan to enter a local competition, the Battle of the Sounds. The story is told in the first person by Paul Crabbe.

The teacher will read an excerpt from the section '1968', starting on page 86 with 'I sat beneath the house of Scotty's absent parents' and ending on page 89 with 'He spits all over you when he's talking.'

8.1 In the opening paragraph the phrase 'the lowest common musical denominator, some crude level at which all the members of the band could participate' indicates that the band members:
  a do not know much about rock'n'roll
  b couldn't play or read music well
  c were not ambitious
  d depended on Rosie.

8.2 The members of the band are:
  a Rosie, Paul, Scotty and Jimmy
  b Rosie, Scotty, Jimmy and Whiteley
  c Paul, Scotty, Jimmy and Reggie
  d Paul, Scotty, Jimmy and Whiteley.

8.3 Slim Dusty is:
  a the judge of the Battle of the Sounds
  b a writer and singer of country and western music
  c a radio announcer in Darwin
  d a member of the band 'Rough Stuff'.

8.4 Decide whether the following statements are true or false.
  a High school students followed Whiteley's program with religious devotion.
  b When Whiteley refuses to play country and western on the radio, the 'hate mail' indicates that his listeners were conservative and moralistic.
  c The hourly country and western track became legendary because Whiteley had had to back down.
  d Whiteley implies that country music is sung through the nose with the mouth shut to keep out the bushflies.
  e Whiteley is the sole adjudicator of the Battle of the Sounds.
  f Whiteley left the south for Darwin because he was involved in a scandal.

8.5 What is the evidence that Paul is:
  a conscious of his image
  b good at playing and writing music
  c enjoying his position in the group.
  Give one example for each.

8.6 What makes this excerpt from the book interesting and entertaining? Make brief notes on characters, language and the situation before writing your final answer.

the OPPOSITE sex

chapter 3

In this chapter you are invited to consider the habits and problems of the opposite sex! Somehow, gender differences have complicated relationships and social issues since time began. This chapter begins with Shakespeare and surveys the hassles of gender relationships across time—and there have always been tensions. First love affairs are always traumatic and puberty blues are not just a phenomenon of the present.

You will be reading:
- a film script
- a drama script
- autobiographies
- a poem
- a novel excerpt
- a personal account
- newspaper feature articles.

You will be writing:
- a film script
- a poetry analysis
- a drama script
- feature articles
- a short story
- an editorial
- a letter to the editor.

1. **DIFFICULT KIDS**
   William Shakespeare
   A Midsummer Night's Dream

2. **AT THE BALL**
   Eleanor Witcombe
   My Brilliant Career: The Screenplay

3. **A ROMANTIC LOVER**
   Oodgeroo of the Tribe Noonuccal (formerly Kath Walker)
   'Gifts'

4. **FIRST LOVE**
   Elizabeth Lane
   Mad as Rabbits

5. **THE END OF AN AFFAIR**
   David Malouf
   Australian Autobiography

6. **FRIENDSHIP RINGS**
   Kathy Lette and Gabrielle Carey
   Puberty Blues

7. **GENDER MATTERS**
   Dale and Lynne Spender
   'Serial partners, multiple careers for the contemporary woman'

   Sally Loane
   'The trouble with boys'

8. Listening
   FIRST DATE DISASTER
   Melina Marchetta
   Looking for Alibrandi

1 DIFFICULT kids

drama script

William Shakespeare
A Midsummer Night's Dream

Throughout time, young men and women have been attracted to one another but 'the course of true love never did run smooth' as William Shakespeare said in his play *A Midsummer Night's Dream*.

BETWEEN THE LINES

1.1 In groups of five, prepare a reading of the drama script on pages 53 and 54, which is from the opening scene of the play. In his palace, the Duke of Athens, Theseus, is looking forward to his wedding to Hippolyta, Queen of the Amazons. Egeus, a citizen, comes to him with a complaint. After reading the drama script in your groups at least twice, complete the following questions and activities.

1.2 Questions in the School Certificate can take this form.

1.2 Read through the following statements and decide whether they are true or false.
  a Egeus is complaining that his daughter, Hermia, does not wish to marry the man of his choice, Demetrius.
  b Theseus orders Hermia to consider her father's rights.
  c Theseus advises Hermia to think about the consequences of disobeying her father.
  d Hermia has to face either death or marriage to Demetrius.
  e Theseus hasn't a good word to say for nuns.
  f Theseus says that those who marry will be happier than those who remain virgins.
  g Demetrius suggests that Lysander is crazy.
  h Egeus says she can think about it until the next new moon.
  i Lysander suggests that Demetrius should marry Egeus.
  j Egeus argues that, as Hermia belongs to him, he has the right to give her to Demetrius.
  k Lysander argues that his greater fortunes are the most important consideration.
  l Lysander suggests that Demetrius has 'made love' to another girl.

1.3 In ten to twelve lines outline the situation described in the extract as clearly as you can. Compare your writing with others in your group.

1.4 Rewrite Egeus' opening greeting in your own words.

(continued p. 55)

ACT 1
SCENE 1. *Athens. The Palace of THESEUS.*
Enter EGEUS, HERMIA, LYSANDER, and DEMETRIUS.

    EGEUS Happy be Theseus, our renowned duke!
    THESEUS Thanks, good Egeus: what's the news with thee?
    EGEUS Full of vexation come I, with complaint
    Against my child, my daughter Hermia.
5   Stand forth, Demetrius. My noble lord,
    This man hath my consent to marry her.
    Stand forth, Lysander: and, my gracious duke,
    This man hath bewitch'd the bosom of my child:
    Thou, thou, Lysander, thou hast given her rimes,
10   And interchang'd love-tokens with my child;
    Thous hast by moonlight at her window sung,
    With feigning voice, verses of feigning love;
    And stol'n the impression of her fantasy
    With bracelets of thy hair, rings, gawds, conceits,
15   Knacks, trifles, nosegays, sweetmeats, messengers
    Of strong prevailment in unharden'd youth;
    With cunning hast thou filch'd my daughter's heart;
    Turn'd her obedience, which is due to me,
    To stubborn harshness. And, my gracious duke,
20   Be it so she will not here before your Grace
    Consent to marry with Demetrius,
    I beg the ancient privilege of Athens,
    As she is mine, I may dispose of her;
    Which shall be either to this gentleman,
25   Or to her death, according to our law
    Immediately provided in that case.
    THESEUS What say you, Hermia? be advis'd, fair maid.
    To you, your father should be as a god;
    One that compos'd your beauties, yea, and one
30   To whom you are but as a form in wax
    By him imprinted, and within his power
    To leave the figure or disfigure it.
    Demetrius is a worthy gentleman.
    HERMIA So is Lysander.
35 **THESEUS** In himself he is;
    But, in this kind, wanting your father's voice,
    The other must be held the worthier.
    HERMIA I would my father look'd but with my eyes.
    THESEUS Rather your eyes must with his judgment look.
40 **HERMIA** I do entreat your Grace to pardon me.
    I know not by what power I am made bold,
    Nor how it may concern my modesty
    In such presence here to plead my thoughts;
    But I beseech your Grace, that I may know
45   The worst that may befall me in this case,
    If I refuse to wed Demetrius.

THESEUS Either to die the death, or to abjure
For ever the society of men.
Therefore fair Hermia, question your desires;
50   Know of your youth, examine well your blood,
Whether, if you yield not to your father's choice,
You can endure the livery of a nun,
For aye to be in shady cloister mew'd,
To live a barren sister all your life,
55   Chanting faint hymns to the cold fruitless moon.
Thrice blessed they that master so their blood,
To undergo such maiden pilgrimage;
But earthlier happy is the rose distill'd,
Than that which withering on the virgin thorn
60   Grows, lives, and dies, in single blessedness.
HERMIA So will I grow, so live, so die, my lord,
Ere I will yield my virgin patent up
Unto his lordship, whose unwished yoke
My soul consents not to give sovereignty.
65 **THESEUS** Take time to pause; and, by the next new moon,—
The sealing-day betwixt my love and me
For everlasting bond of fellowship,—
Upon that day either prepare to die
For disobedience to your father's will,
70   Or else to wed Demetrius, as he would;
Or on Diana's altar to protest
For aye austerity and single life.
DEMETRIUS Relent, sweet Hermia; and, Lysander, yield
Thy crazed title to my certain right.
75 **LYSANDER** You have her father's love, Demetrius;
Let me have Hermia's: do you marry him.
EGEUS Scornful Lysander! true, he hath my love,
And what is mine my love shall render him;
And she is mine, and all my right of her
80   I do estate unto Demetrius.
LYSANDER I am, my lord, as well deriv'd as he,
As well possess'd; my love is more than his;
My fortunes every way as fairly rank'd
If not with vantage, as Demetrius';
85   And, which is more than all these boasts can be,
I am belov'd of beauteous Hermia.
Why should not I then prosecute my right?
Demetrius, I'll avouch it to his head,
Made love to Nedar's daughter, Helena,
90   And won her soul; and she, sweet lady, dotes,
Devoutly dotes, dotes in idolatry,
Upon this spotted and inconstant man.

1.5 The word closest in meaning to 'vexation', as it is used in this excerpt (line 3), is:
   a irritation
   b depression
   c anger
   d despair.

1.6 Shakespeare uses words such as 'hath', 'thou' and 'rimes' and phrases such as 'happy be' and 'what say you?' because:
   a that is the language he used
   b he is using incorrect language
   c he is trying to sound impressive
   d he is trying to sound like the Bible.

1.7 'This man hath bewitch'd the bosom of my child' (line 8) means:
   a Lysander has thrown a spell on Egeus' daughter
   b Demetrius and Hermia have fallen in love
   c Lysander is so attractive to Hermia that she has fallen in love with him
   d Lysander is desperately attracted to Hermia.

1.8 'With feigning voice, verses of feigning love' (line 12) suggests that:
   a Lysander's songs are faint
   b Lysander has written verses and sung songs to impress Hermia
   c Lysander's poetry is not his own
   d Lysander's love is not genuine.

1.9 In groups, write multiple-choice questions about the meaning of 'Of strong prevailment in unharden'd youth' (line 16) and 'filch'd' (line 17). Peer assess the questions.

> **1.9** Refer to the Appendix for guidelines on multiple-choice questions.

1.10 Explain in four or five lines what the 'ancient privilege of Athens' (line 22) might be.

1.11 Theseus says Hermia should see her father as a god (line 28) because:
   a Egeus is her biological father and is responsible for her beauty
   b Hermia is subject to her father's good will and wishes
   c Egeus can ruin her life
   d all of the above.

1.12 Explain the reasons for your answer to question 1.11 and use quotations to support your reasons.

1.13 Describe the life of a nun in your own words. Refer to lines 52–5.

1.14 Write eight or ten lines explaining the meaning of lines 56–60.

1.15 In ten or twelve lines explain whether you think Lysander's final speech is an example of a sound, well-structured argument or a biased, hysterical outburst.

> **1.15** Refer to the Appendix for guidelines on argument and speech.

2 at the BALL

film script

Eleanor Witcombe
My Brilliant Career: The Screenplay

A ball is often used in stories as the setting for the climax of emotions between lovers.

> 76. INT. FIVE BOB DINING ROOM. NIGHT
> HARRY *sits at the top of a large table. On his right is MISS DERRICK, who is monopolising the conversation.*
> *Farther down the table the elderly gentleman GUEST is talking to*
> 5 SYBYLLA *but her eyes are on HARRY and MISS DERRICK.*
> *Snatches of conversation regarding wool prices, the weather etc. emerge, while the guests are being served.*
> UNCLE J.J.: I see that Furlow has bought himself a very fine bull.
> *(Opposite, SYBYLLA looks up.)*
> 10 SYBYLLA: *(Loudly: unable to help herself)* That should make a few cows happy!
> *(There is a brief pause. The elderly gentleman GUEST beside her tries to stifle a laugh. MISS DERRICK looks down her nose. GRANDMOTHER, opposite, exchanges an agonised glance with AUNT HELEN.*
> 15 AUNT GUSSIE *can't suppress a small, carefully restrained smile.*
> HARRY *looks at* SYBYLLA. SHE *meets his eye blandly.)*
> [*While the Beechams entertain their guests with music, reading and conversation in the main house, Sybylla prefers the company of the employees in the woolshed.*]
> 79. EXT. FIVE BOB YARD. NIGHT
> *The sound of the bush band playing traditional dance tunes comes from the woolshed.*
> 20 *Around the bonfire, children are playing and groups of guests stand talking, laughing and drinking.*
> SYBYLLA *stalks past them, unnoticed, towards the woolshed.*

Sybylla writes a letter home while working for the McSwats.

80. INT. THE WOOLSHED. NIGHT

It is gay with streamers, flowering wattle branches, and young gum tips, and hanging lamps.

A small BUSH BAND of fiddle, concertina, bush-bass, bones and banjo are playing a vigorous tune—such as 'Eubalong Ball'—to which the Five Bob 'hands' and staff and those from neighbouring properties are dancing vigorously and with open enjoyment...

At the other end of the shed are trestle tables on which a lavish amount of food is being arranged by some of the women.

Nobody notices as SYBYLLA comes in. SHE sees JOE, a Five Bob hand, and goes to him. He grins at her.

JOE: How are you going, miss? Having a good time?

SYBYLLA: Will you dance with me?

JOE: Righto.

(He hands his drink to someone, and they move onto the floor and join in the dancing.)

SYBYLLA: They're too stuffy back there.

JOE: Forgotten how to enjoy themselves. *(He sings with the tune)* 'I look upon the nobles with their lineages old...' Know Henry Lawson?

(SYBYLLA grins and sings the next line as she dances.)

SYBYLLA: 'I looked upon their mansions and their acres and their gold...'

JOE: *(Singing)* 'I saw their women radiant in jewelled gowns appear...'

JOE and SYBYLLA: *(Singing together)* 'And then I joined the army of the outcasts in the rear...'

(Laughing together, they whirl around the floor... as uninhibited as the rest.

Led by HARRY and AUNT GUSSIE, the GUESTS arrive to watch. Some chairs have been arranged for them on the edge of the floor.

AUNT GUSSIE motions GRANDMOTHER to sit beside her. Some, including UNCLE J.J. with MISS DERRICK, join in the dancing.

HARRY sourly watches SYBYLLA dancing with JOE.

GRANDMOTHER also sees, with dismay, and draws AUNT HELEN's attention. AUNT GUSSIE follows their gaze—and looks amused.

HARRY, with mounting anger, pushes through the dances and tries to cut in, tapping JOE on the shoulder. JOE doesn't seem to notice—and they wheel away. HARRY follows as SYBYLLA swings out from JOE, he seizes her and pulls her aside roughly ... leading her through the dancers towards the door.

AUNT GUSSIE notices with some concern.)

81. EXT. FIVE BOB YARD/HOUSE. NIGHT

Beyond the bonfire, SYBYLLA is struggling with HARRY.

SYBYLLA: Let me go!

(HARRY ignores her, dragging her after him

The characters are (from left to right) Sybylla Melvyn, Frank Hawden (the English jackeroo), Grandmother and Harry Beecham.

towards the house. HE opens a side door and pushes SYBYLLA in to
75 *what is evidently his office.)*

82. INT. HARRY'S OFFICE. NIGHT

HARRY pushes SYBYLLA in and turns to close the door. It is a working manager's room with HARRY'S paraphernalia around. HIS riding crop is on the desk on top of accounts and papers.

80   *HE lets go of SYBYLLA who is furious.*

SYBYLLA: Didn't you like me dancing with the peasants? I'm one of them, you know.

HARRY: *(Quietly furious)* I'm not going to make a long yarn of this...

85 SYBYLLA: Shocked you, did I?

HARRY: In a few days I have to go away...

SYBYLLA: Oh, more shearing somewhere else?
(SHE picks up the riding crop, unconsciously, and plays with it.)

HARRY: ...and I must be told is it yes or no?

90 SYBYLLA: What's the question?

HARRY: I thought...I thought we might get married.
(SYBYLLA is taken by surprise and hesitates a moment. Then she flares back at him.)

SYBYLLA: *(Mocking him)* Well, what a handsome proposal! How
95   could anyone say no?
(At the end of his tether, HARRY grabs her.)

HARRY: *(Grating it out!)* How dare you!
(HARRY suddenly pulls her to him as though he is going to kiss her roughly.

100   *SYBYLLA raises the riding crop and slashes HARRY across the face. HARRY, stunned, steps back putting his hand to his cheek. SYBYLLA stands, appalled at herself.*
A beat—and HARRY wrenches the crop from her and throws it aside. HE puts a handkerchief to his cheek.
105   *SYBYLLA doesn't know what to say.)*

SYBYLLA: Harry, I'm...I'm...I didn't...

HARRY: *(Quietly)* My fault...It was stupid of me...I really should get back to my guests.
(He turns and goes out.
110   *SYBYLLA looks after him, shattered by what she has done. Tears run down her face.)*

BETWEEN THE LINES

The previous scenes are from the film script of *My Brilliant Career*. While staying on her uncle's country property, Sybylla Melvyn, the daughter of a poor farmer, is reacquainted with her cousin, Harry Beecham, who is the owner of the adjoining property, Five Bob Downs. They are immediately attracted to one another, but at a ball given by Harry, Sybylla finds she has a rival, Miss Derrick, who is possibly a more suitable and conventional match for Harry. Sybylla's response is to snub Harry and behave as though she doesn't care.

2.1 In your own words, explain the information given immediately after scene 76, that is, 'INT. FIVE BOB DINING ROOM. NIGHT'.

2.2 In scene 76, when Sybylla makes her loud remark about the cows, what do the reactions of the people at the dinner table tell you about the attitudes of people in the 1890s? Consider the reaction of each character mentioned before writing your answer.

2.3 In your own words, explain the meaning of the song that Joe and Sybylla sing (lines 40–9). How does the song indicate Sybylla's feelings?

> **2.3** Remember to have your dictionary handy at all times.

2.4 Why does Grandmother watch Sybylla dancing with Joe 'with dismay' (line 57)?

2.5 Scenes 81 and 82 involve only Sybylla and Harry. Why do you think that Scene 81 is separated from scene 82?

2.6 Research the word 'peasants'. It is not a word commonly used in Australia to describe workers. Why do you think Sybylla uses it in scene 82?

2.7 'I'm not going to make a long yarn of this...' (lines 72–3). In this context, 'a long yarn' probably means:
 a an elaborate lie
 b a complicated tale
 c a long speech
 d a lengthy discussion.

2.8 Explain Sybylla's response to Harry's proposal, 'I thought we might get married' (line 90).

2.9 Why do you think Harry proposes in such a way?

2.10 Ask your teacher to show you, on video, the scene from *Pride and Prejudice* by Jane Austen, where Mr Darcy proposes to Elizabeth Bennet.

> **2.10** BBC Television made a television series of *Pride and Prejudice*. It is available on video. The scene you need to watch appears at the end of episode 4. Alternatively your teacher could read chapter 34 of the novel to the class.

2.11 Compare the *Pride and Prejudice* excerpt (see activity 2.10, above) with the excerpt from the film script of *My Brilliant Career*. Make notes on the setting, the language and the characters, including their attitudes and reasoning and their feelings at the conclusion of the scene. Write about one and a half pages.

2.12 Compare the drama script in Unit 1 (pp. 56–8), and some modern drama scripts, with this film script. On the basis of the comparison, list two or three differences between drama scripts and film scripts.

> **2.12** Your teacher will be able to show you examples of other drama scripts.

2.13 Writing
In the introduction to the film script of *My Brilliant Career*, Eleanor Witcombe says a scriptwriter needs to remember that the 'one camera shot can cover pages of the book.' With this in mind, write the script for the scene in the photograph on page 57, which is a still from the film. Remember to set out your film script exactly as shown in the excerpt, detailing first the scene number, whether it is an interior or exterior shot, the setting and the time of day. You will need to write detailed directions and some conversation. Before you begin, study the photograph carefully and make notes about the

2.14 A voice-over is a scene where the character is not seen to speak, but we hear his or her voice or the voice of a narrator.

2.14 Remember to set out your script correctly.

occasion, the way the characters are dressed, their expressions and attitudes and where each character is looking.

2.14 Writing
During her stay on her uncle's property, Sybylla learns that her alcoholic father is once more in debt and she must become a governess to the McSwat's unruly children. Write the script, a 'voice-over', for the photograph of Sybylla on page 56, which is another still from the film. The voice-over could be Sybylla reading as she writes or it could be the voice of a narrator or one of the children looking through the window.

3 a ROMANTIC lover

poem

Oodgeroo of the Tribe Noonuccal (formerly Kath Walker) 'Gifts'

Romance is not dead.

BETWEEN THE LINES

Read the poem on page 61 and then complete the following activities.

3.1 Questions in the School Certificate can take this form.

3.1 Copy out the following short response to the poem, replacing the numbered space with the most suitable alternative provided for that number.

In this poem, a young man offers the young woman he loves presents (such as pendants and decorative feathers), a child, protection, 'remembered songs' and romance. She shakes her head and is [**3.2**]. She merely wishes for tree-grubs, which she probably considers [**3.3**].

The poem is expressed in [**3.4**] language. In the first stanza, love is equated with light, colour and movement. [**3.5**]

The second stanza suggests that his love will bring her a child and that he will protect and provide for her. The image of a 'great rain-maker' suggests [**3.6**]. He also promises that she will be remembered in songs 'in all the wandering camps', which suggests that [**3.7**].

Finally the lover offers images of beauty such as moonlight, birdsong, stars and 'the bright rainbow'. To her these promises are [**3.8**].

The short lines between each stanza indicate the young woman's responses, which are simple and direct and create a contrast to the romantic ideas of her lover. The poem leaves the reader feeling [**3.9**].

> 'I will bring you love,' said the young lover,
> 'A glad light to dance in your dark eye.
> Pendants I will bring of the white bone,
> And gay parrot feathers to deck your hair.'
>
> 5 But she only shook her head.
>
> 'I will put a child in your arms,' he said.
> 'Will be a great headman, great rain-maker.
> I will make remembered songs about you
> That all the tribes in all the wandering camps
> 10 Will sing for ever.'
>
> But she was not impressed.
>
> 'I will bring you the still moonlight of the lagoon
> And steal for you the singing of all the birds;
> I will bring down the stars of heaven to you,
> 15 And put the bright rainbow into your hand.'
>
> 'No,' she said, 'bring me tree-grubs.'
>
> Oodgeroo of the Tribe Noonuccal,
> Pamela Allardice (ed.), *The Language of Love:*
> *An Anthology of Australian Love Letters, Poetry and Prose*

3.2 **a** unmoved
　　b scornful
　　c irritated
　　d angry

3.3 **a** delicious
　　b practical
　　c more appropriate
　　d all of the above

3.4 **a** ordinary and mundane
　　b pathetic
　　c simple and lyrical
　　d colloquial

3.5 Write five or six lines containing examples to support the statement: 'his love is equated with light, colour and movement.'

3.6 **a** fantasy
　　b fertility and growth
　　c too much rain
　　d a lot of dancing

3.7 **a** the Aborigines are nomadic
　　b only wanderers sing songs
　　c camp sites are good for singing
　　d her fame will spread across the land

3.8
  a silly and unrealistic
  b colourful
  c a metaphoric expression of his love
  d fantastical and grand

3.9
  a sad because the romantic gestures of the lover have been rejected
  b amused because the young woman is so practical
  c moved by the beauty of the images
  d bored by the subject matter

3.9 There is no 'right' answer to this question. Your choice depends on your response to the poem. You may wish to include two or three of the suggested responses in your answer.

3.10 Explain the reasons for your answer to 3.9.

4 FIRST love

autobiography

Elizabeth Lane
Mad as Rabbits

Elizabeth Lane grew up during the Depression on a farm in Victoria. In her autobiography, *Mad as Rabbits*, she recalls spying, scrub style, on her sister Marg's 'affair' with Pimple-face.

BETWEEN THE LINES

Read the autobiography on page 63 and then complete the following questions and activities.

4.1 The mushrooming expedition (line 2) is:
  a an expedition that is getting bigger
  b a walk with friends on a sunny day
  c an excursion to collect mushrooms
  d a Sunday outing.

4.2 The writer (Elizabeth Lane) and Marj would have separated so that:
  a Elizabeth could return to Ann
  b they could find more mushrooms
  c they could go in different directions
  d Marj could return to Ann.

4.3 Definitions of 'slang' and 'colloquial language' appear in the Key Terms section of the Appendix.

4.3 The word 'scrub' (line 4) is an example of:
  a the wrong word
  b colloquial language
  c inappropriate language
  d slang.

(continued p. 64)

One Sunday when toothache had kept Ann home from the mushrooming expedition, I turned back and followed Marj when we separated. Before she'd gone very far, she turned and hurried into the scrub.

Nobody with any sense ever went mushrooming in scrub, so I immediately grinned to myself. And when I saw a pimple-faced lad who had attended every Salvation Army rally come out of the scrub to meet her, I knew my suspicions were justified.

I made a detour around the paddock, and then, fencepost by fencepost, bush by bush, I crept, stalked and wriggled until I was safely sheltered in an umbrella-bush about ten yards from where they sat on a log at the edge of the scrub.

I wished I had Ann there to giggle with me. The young man told Marj she had the most beautiful eyes in the world; and she gazed into his face with wide-open eyes, not once referring to his pimples, which I felt was unfair, considering that she was forever throwing off at our boys about pimples...

When I heard him tell Marj that he would leave a note for her in the hollow of the big strainer-post on the corner of the paddock on Wednesday I nearly laughed out loud. Then I wriggled, crept and stalked, bush by bush, fencepost by fencepost, until I was back in the open paddock again. I was impatient to race home and tell Ann, but when Marj and I met in the open paddock, each innocently swinging an empty billy, I suddenly felt many years older than Ann and closer to Marj, and how glad I was that Marj did have the most beautiful eyes in the world...

All the same, this feeling of closeness to Marj didn't stop me from making a round trip past the hollow strainer-post on my way to school on Wednesday and lifting the promised note from it.

At playtime I took Renie Bryce into the seclusion of the wattle tree and showed her the letter.

'Eyes like stars! Lips ripe for love!' How we giggled over those tender passages.

I replaced the letter on the way home from school, but from the way Marj looked at me after that I knew she was aware I had discovered her romance.

That summer we still went mushrooming, even when it was no longer the season for mushrooms, Ann being outmanoeuvred before we left the house.

When we 'accidentally' met Pimple-face, who was also busy mushrooming out of season, I would leave them and—feeling I now knew all the intricacies of courting, and considering them rather silly—gladly wander off in the scrub and enjoy myself collecting different sorts of grubs and caterpillars, and eating wattle-gum, or lying on my back, hands pillowing my head, working out pictures in the different cloud-formations—whiling away a pleasant hour or two before rejoining Marj.

Pamela Allardice (ed.), *The Language of Love: An Anthology of Australian Love Letters, Poetry and Prose*

4.4 Pimple-face probably 'attended every Salvation Army rally' (line 7) because:
  a he was a devout Christian
  b Marj and her sisters attended and he wanted to see Marj
  c he was an enthusiastic follower of the Salvation Army
  d he liked the excitement of rally driving.

> **4.5** Read the question very carefully.

4.5 The most unlikely reason for Marj 'not once referring to his pimples' (lines 15–16) is that:
  a pimples do not matter when you are in love
  b she was more interested in her effect on him
  c she did not want to embarrass him
  d she did not see them.

4.6 'Each innocently swinging an empty billy' (lines 23–4) indicates that:
  a both girls were pretending there were no mushrooms
  b neither girl had been able to find any mushrooms
  c neither girl had wanted to find mushrooms
  d both girls were too silly to find mushrooms.

4.7 Elizabeth feels 'closer to Marj' (line 25) because she:
  a is much older than Ann
  b is envious of Marj's romance
  c feels closer to Marj than she did before
  d wants to find out more about love.

4.8 Elizabeth takes the note left by Pimple-face because she is:
  a curious
  b jealous
  c concerned
  d a nasty child.

> **4.9** A definition of 'cliché' appears in the Key Terms section of the Appendix.

4.9 '"Eyes like stars! Lips ripe for love!"' are referred to as 'tender passages' (line 32) because:
  a the expressions are clichés
  b they are weak expressions
  c eyes and lips are tender and delicate
  d the boy is expressing delicate feelings.

4.10 In this context, 'outmanoeuvred' (line 38) probably means Ann was:
  a forced to stay home
  b tricked into staying home
  c asked to stay home
  d left behind.

4.11 The 'intricacies of courting' (line 42) refers to:
  a trying to win the affections of a woman
  b meeting someone of the opposite sex in private
  c the complicated rituals of attracting someone
  d complex plans.

4.12 The attitude of the author to these childhood experiences could best be described as:
- **a** affectionate and amused
- **b** superior and scornful
- **c** light-hearted and cheerful
- **d** personal and serious.

5 the END of an affair

David Malouf
Australian Autobiography

autobiography

The intricacies of courting were just as complicated ten to twenty years later. David Malouf recalls a painful experience.

BETWEEN THE LINES

Read the autobiography on page 66 and then complete the following questions and activities.

5.1 In groups, discuss the setting of this piece of writing. Write down the details of language and action that suggest the setting of the story.

5.2 Explain the effectiveness of the simile used in the first sentence.

5.3 Research 'mint juleps', 'malteds' and 'Gipsy Tap'.

5.4 Express the phrase 'retained something of its wartime glamour and notoriety' (line 7) in your own words.

5.5 What is Malouf implying about the waitress when he describes her as looking 'as if she might remember the place in the old days' (lines 9–10)?

5.6 In groups, study the guidelines on narrative structure and then identify how Malouf's story conforms to the structure.

5.7 Write eight or ten lines explaining how the introductory sentence establishes the situation and suggests why Roseanne is attractive.

5.8 What is the complication and how does Malouf react? Which events develop the plot and characterisation?

5.9 Identify the crisis or turning point in the story.

5.10 Identify the resolution. How does it represent a development of understanding on the part of the central character?

5.1 Refer to the Appendix for guidelines on setting.

5.2 A definition of 'simile' appears in the Key Terms section of the Appendix.

5.6 TO 5.10 Refer to the Appendix for guidelines on narrative structure.

> I had fallen heavily in my last year for a Somerville House girl called Roseanne Staples, who wore nylon stockings that shifted their lights like mother of pearl and was a GPS diving champion. All one Wednesday at Moss's, and again the next, we danced dreamily under the rafters and I took her afterwards for mint
> 5 juleps and malteds at the Pig 'n Whistle, a milk bar at the top of town that had been a favourite pick-up place for American soldiers and retained something of its wartime glamour and notoriety. It was regarded as daring and I was out to impress. When the waitress, who looked as if she might remember the place in the old
> 10 days, slid our milk-shakes down the glass-topped counter, she winked in the direction of the innocent Roseanne and whispered: 'There y'are love. That'll put lead in yer pencil.' I could hardly wait for the week to pass. But on the third Wednesday, as we went whirling across the floor in what seemed to be a most
> 15 accomplished manner, Roseanne, with a casualness that astonishes me even today, it was so low-keyed, so undramatic, pronounced the words that put an end to our affair, pfft! just like that, and changed the course of my life. Looking straight over my shoulder, in the most neutral tones: 'If there's one thing I can't stand,' said
> 20 Roseanne Staples, slowly, 'it's boys who don't pivot.'
>   I was thunderstruck. The pivot—that little sidestep and pass at the corner of the floor that I had never quite got the knack of, it seemed so silly, hardly worth worrying about. I smiled wanly and guided her through the rest of the set, closing my eyes and
> 25 swallowing hard as we approached the corners and wishing Moss's was triangular. *Four* corners was suddenly more than I could bear. Back safe among the boys I waited for something less subtle, like a Gipsy Tap…
>
> Pamela Allardice (ed.) *The Language of Love: An Anthology of Love Letters, Poetry and Prose*

6 FRIENDSHIP rings

personal account

Kathy Lette and Gabrielle Carey
Puberty Blues

When *Puberty Blues* was published in 1979, many readers were shocked by its honest description of life in Sydney's southern suburbs.

Bruce Board was tall, blond and drove a panel van. He'd left school early, like some of the boys in the gang. He was a top guy, 'cause he had money, a car and a brand new board. Now all he needed was a brand new chick.

5   Bruce and I sauntered towards each other. The gang circled the chosen two, jeering and prodding.

'Go get 'er, Brew.'

'Kiss 'er, Boardie. Go on.' The ring closed in around us. My heart was thumping.

10   'Come on ... We're waitin'...'

'Rip in Brew. Don't be shy ...' Sneer, snigger. This was it. He took me by the shoulders and we kissed.

'Yyyaaay.'

'Ooooh. Wooo.' Whistle.

15   'We're goin' for a walk,' he told me, leading me off to the bushes by the hand.

'It only takes ten minutes,' called out Strack after us. The boys roared with laughter.

Behind the lantana we kissed again.

20   'Will you go round wiv me?' he said.

And that was the courting ceremony in Sylvania Heights, where I grew up. Everyone was going around with somebody. If a guy didn't have a girlfriend, he'd just pick one from a distance. Someone about his height, his hair colour, not too fat, not too skinny and always wearing a

25   pair of straight-legged Levis...

Getting a friendship ring was the biggest thing in a girl's life. If you had a ring you were a top chick. Girls rushed up to you every day at school.

'Give us a look. Oh ... is it 18-carat?'

30   'Yeah, have a look.'

'Oh gee he treats ya good. It's bewdiful.'

'Yeah he treats me roolly good and stuff.'

'How long have you been goin' round with 'im now?'

'Three months, two weeks, four days and um ... what's the time? ...

35   two hours.'

'Whenja get it?'

> 'Saturday night.'
> On the way home from your boyfriend's place, just after he'd given you a ring, you'd pause under the street light and examine it. Was it 18-
> 40 carat? ... Phew ...
> By day, we were at school learning logarithms but by night—in the back of cars, under the bowling alleys, on Cronulla Beach, down behind the Ace of Spades Hotel, in the changing rooms of the football field, or, if you were lucky, in a bed while someone's parents were out—you paid
> 45 off your friendship ring.

BETWEEN THE LINES

6.1 You should consider such features as word choice, use of dialogue and tone.

6.1 Refer to the Appendix for guidelines on style and tone.

6.3 Refer to the Appendix for guidelines on drama scripts.

6.1 This excerpt from *Puberty Blues* is different in style from the previous readings in this chapter. Write down three features of the style of this piece which illustrate how it is different and give examples.

6.2 Writing
As a feature writer for a newspaper, you have been asked by the editor to write an entertaining feature article about teenage relationships for the weekend edition. You decide to explore relationships at different stages in history. Write your article based on the material so far in this chapter and any other material you choose. Write about 500 to 600 words.

6.3 Writing
Write a drama script based on the excerpt from Elizabeth Lane's autobiography, *Mad as Rabbits* (p. 64). Have a play reading for the rest of the class.

6.4 Writing
Write your own short script or short story, depicting a conflict in the relationship between two young lovers.

7 gender MATTERS

newspaper feature article

Dale and Lynne Spender
'Serial partners, multiple careers for the contemporary woman'

During the twentieth century, many things have changed for women and men. The following controversial articles suggest some of the ways conditions in society have changed and how this may affect young people of both sexes.

Serial partners, multiple careers for the contemporary woman

1 The way society is travelling these days, young women should prepare themselves for two facts of life: they will probably have several careers ... and more than one husband. Sisters *Dale* and *Lynne Spender* offer some advice.

2 Once upon a time, the only thing a girl had to do was find Prince Charming—and she would be set for the rest of her life. She didn't need to worry her pretty little head about earning her own living or supporting children. Quite the opposite.

3 But the fairytale is over. These days a sensible girl has to think about making it on her own. So it's no longer diamonds that are a girl's best friend, but sound career advice.

4 And this is where we have something of a problem. It isn't just the women's role that has changed so dramatically; work has also been revolutionised.

5 Parents, teachers and even politicians know that technology is changing the job scene, but the best some professionals can do is pronounce that 'most of the jobs of the next century haven't even been invented yet.' This is not much help to those trying to plan for their working life and financial security ...

6 Here's the clue for making sense of it all. We are no longer an industrial society: we are rapidly becoming an information-based one, with very different notions of wealth, very different demands for skills and very different work patterns ...

> So it's no longer diamonds that are a girl's best friend, but sound career advice.

7 Besides, we shouldn't keep kidding ourselves that jobs are the only way—or even the best way—to structure work. No-one wanted to work in factories when these jobs arrived. And some of the jobs that are going today are not all that pleasant, either ...

8 The biggest change is from the regimented jobs in office or factory to flexible, part-time temporary contract or consultancy work. Instead of being employed by someone and going off each day to a central place of work for a regulation number of hours, you are more likely to be doing a few jobs—and working for yourself.

9 It's the portfolio, or serial, pattern of employment.

10 Young people are already making the adjustments. They don't expect to just finish school, do their training and have a job for life, as their parents did. They don't even find such a prospect attractive.

11 'Did you really think you'd get a degree and do the same job for forty years?' they may ask their elders in amazement.

12 They know they will train and retrain and retrain: they plan to do many jobs throughout their working lives. And they don't have the older generation's hang-ups about status.

13 'My job in the computer industry will only last a couple of years,' said one bright young woman. 'But then I wouldn't mind spending some time in the hospitality industry—on a resort island.'

14 After that? It could be time for something different ...

15 Skills are changing so quickly in the information economy that daily learning will soon be as familiar to us as daily work. This means there will be a big demand for learning agencies that can deliver skills on-line, and just in time, for the next paying task.

16 It is indeed a revolution. It means that most of us will be responsible for our own work.

In the information society we will be more like individual small businesses—and very much on our own.

17   So the best career advice is to get an education in self-management. And computer competence is a must.

18   Women today are likely to spend more years in the workplace than their grandmothers expected to live. But not in one career. Indeed, if you haven't registered from one source or another that your current job will be obsolete in five years—and if you haven't started retraining—then you haven't been paying attention.

19   But it's still not quite kosher to plan serial relationships (which brings the same sort of reaction as discussing serial murders). Somehow, relationships are just supposed to happen. Like you FALL in love. Unplanned, out of the blue. To acknowledge that you might have prepared for a relationship as you would for a career or a job is to leave yourself open to be accused by him—and his mates, and probably his family—of being a manipulative and scheming wench.

20   But to rely on hormones alone in your choice of partners does not sit well with the blueprint of the life of a serious contemporary woman ...

21   Statistically, we know that one in three marriages will break up in the first seven years and with the most inevitable disappointments and traumas. Why take the risk? Better to plan your first serious relationship as a non-marital one. Choose someone who is fun, a bit irresponsible, interesting and sexy. It allows you to be the same ...

22   When you are ready for a period of commitment and Saturday night videos rather than rave parties, it's time to plan for a second relationship.

> **Ideally, you should be about forty-five and the partner a good ten years younger.**

23   Marriage at this stage can be appealing. Look for someone steadier—even a bit serious and preferably with money in the bank. It should be someone equally interested in nest-building, parenting ... and housework.

24   This is the time to have children. If the chosen partner has some money to add to yours, you have genuine choices about continuing to work in paid employment. And if he's interested in the house and housework, you may be able to avoid some of the pitfalls of contemporary heterosexual relationships.

25   Studies of such relationships—regardless of the politics of the researchers—indicated that you will do more housework and get less sleep than your partner. Whether or not you work outside the home, primary responsibility for the shopping, cleaning, cooking, washing and child care are all likely to be yours.

26   If you decide on marriage, a prenuptial agreement is essential. Clever girls will include agreements to cover domestic arrangement as well as financial ones.

27   As the kids reach independence—somewhere between five and twenty-five—it's time to keep an eye out for the next partner. Someone quite a few years younger. Take stock of the fact that you are likely to live until you're eighty plus—and you don't want to do it on your own. Men have a horrible habit of dying earlier than women, so your chances with a partner your own age are that he'll either die before you or he'll become sick and you'll have to look after him. The idea of spending years visiting him in a nursing home until you are so worn out that you have to enter one yourself is not an attractive one.

28   You can avoid this by selecting a younger partner who admires your wit and wisdom and who is happy to offer caring and sharing in return. Ideally, you should be about forty-five and the partner a good ten years younger. It might involve a little investment with a plastic surgeon for a nip and tuck but this is a small price to pay.

29   Seriously, it simply doesn't make sense to adapt to changing work patterns while coyly leaving relationships to fate, romance or hormones. A critical mass of scheming wenches could turn this tide and make it perfectly acceptable for women to plan multiple careers—and carefully select serial partners.

Sun-Herald, 29 March 1998

BETWEEN THE LINES

7.1 The phrase that is closest in meaning to 'serial' (title) in this context is:
  a something published or broadcast in instalments
  b one after another
  c a number of things out of order
  d breakfast food.

7.2 This excerpt is a:
  a fairy tale
  b child's story
  c feature article
  d legend.

7.3 'Once upon a time' (paragraph 2) is used to suggest:
  a that women's lives were like a fairy tale existence
  b that all women always lived happily every after
  c that women who marry will live like princesses
  d the contrast between women's lives then and now.

7.4 'She didn't need to worry her pretty little head' (paragraph 2) implies that:
  a pretty girls would have been worried if they thought about anything
  b girls only needed to be pretty and someone else would worry
  c girls did not need to worry if they were pretty
  d pretty girls did not think.

7.5 'Most of the jobs of the next century haven't even been invented yet' (paragraph 5) is an example of:
  a a conundrum
  b stupidity
  c sarcasm
  d a pun.

7.5 Use your dictionary and write definitions of these words before answering the question.

7.6 Use your dictionary to find the meaning of 'industrial' and then write a definition of 'industrial society' (paragraph 6). Make sure you avoid using the words 'industrial' and 'industry'.

7.7 'It's the portfolio, or serial, pattern of employment' (paragraph 9) refers to:
  a a new way of working
  b a precarious way of working
  c choosing different jobs at random
  d working at a variety of different jobs in turn.

7.8 Identify four important changes in work conditions from paragraphs 15–18.

7.9 A definition of 'colloquial language' appears in the Key Terms section of the Appendix.

7.9 In paragraph 19 'kosher' is used because:
   a the article is about Jewish people
   b the writers have used the wrong word
   c the writers are using 'kosher' as a colloquial expression
   d 'kosher' means 'correct'.

7.10 'Like you FALL in love. Unplanned, out of the blue' (paragraph 19) implies that:
   a you are unlikely to fall in love
   b the writers are scornful about love
   c this is not a wise idea
   d planning is not acceptable.

7.11 Rewrite paragraph 20 in your own words.

7.12 Outline the three types of relationships that are discussed in paragraphs 20 to 29.

7.13 Refer to the Appendix for guidelines on letters.

7.13 Writing
In groups, discuss the issues raised in this article and then write a letter to the editor of the newspaper expressing your views.
Begin your letter, Dear Editor.
OR
Write an editorial on 'The Contemporary Woman'.

---

newspaper feature article

Sally Loane
'The trouble with boys'

While girls are gradually gaining more self-assurance and freedom, boys have been exhibiting some different and interesting behaviour patterns.

BETWEEN THE LINES

Read the newspaper feature article on pages 73 and 74 and then complete the following questions and activities.

7.14 Paragraph 2 begins: 'Boys are trouble.' In your own words, explain why.

7.15 'Boys are *in* trouble' (paragraph 3). Using the information in paragraphs 3 to 7, summarise the reasons why.

7.16 Identify the five experts whose opinions are expressed in the article. Write down the most important idea you think each expert contributes to the article.

7.17 Discuss the issues raised in the article. Paragraphs 14 and 15 suggest that there is a relationship between the problems of girls and boys. Do you agree?

7.18 What criticisms are made of schools and teachers? Do you think they are fair? Why or why not?

7.19 Writing
Prepare an article for your school newspaper in which you suggest ways in which the problems and difficulties discussed in the article can be addressed in your school and/or community.

The trouble with boys

by Sally Loane

1   When a group of teenage boys ambles into view, a baggy-shirted, pimpled, skateboard-carrying mob fairly pulsating with nonchalance and aggression, we avoid eye contact and cross the street. No matter that they could be our sons, our grandsons, our patients, our students, harmless and lovable kids out for a stroll. Their presence stirs something deep and primal. Fear.

2   Boys are trouble. Boys are scary. Boys are toxic. In the US, according to a report in the *Los Angeles Times Magazine*, the American boy has become so frightening that many States are moving to lower the age when criminal defendants can be tried as adults.

3   Boys are *in* trouble. Boys commit suicide at a rate that has pushed Australia's youth suicide rate up to the second highest in the world. Boys are overwhelmingly more likely than girls to die in car smashes, [to] be convicted for assault and to die from accidents like falls and drownings. It is the boys from the bottom of the class who are more likely to turn up in the morgues and hospital casualty sections.

4   Boys beat girls hands down at drug and alcohol abuse, burns, expulsions from school, reading difficulties, behavioural problems, low literacy, low self-esteem, spinal cord damage and head injuries.

> *Best thing about being male:*
> Stand up to wee.
> Good at picnics.
> Always [have] a mother to look after them.
> *Worst thing:*
> Hairy bodies.
> Discouraged from showing caring.
>
> Views of teenage boys in *Boys in Schools*.

5   In the past decade boys have slipped behind girls in academic performance and school retention rates. Boys sit on the sidelines. Overwhelmingly fewer boys take part in leadership programs, school councils, debating teams, exchange programs. Duke of Edinburgh awards, cultural programs, school choirs and liturgical and canteen duties.

6   Nine times more boys than girls suffer from attention deficit disorder (or ADD, once called hyperactivity). In the US the manufacture of the drug Ritalin, a stimulant which controls fidgeting and hyperactivity, has increased by 300 per cent in the past five years. Here, too, there has been a surge in ADD cases and medication use.

7   There are nine times more boys than girls in detention classes in schools across the State [NSW] and nine times more boys than girls are referred to experts for emotional and behavioural problems. More boys are colour blind, have speech impediments and hearing difficulties. Despite several years of safe sex education, the latest figures show that young men are continuing to become infected with HIV/AIDS.

8   'If these health statistics were affecting any other group in our society, it would be identified as a crisis; the group would have a chorus of advocates and governments would fall over themselves to set up

inquiries,' said Richard Fletcher, an academic and male health educator.

9 'We tell boys for twenty years that they're no good, they're useless and dangerous and we wonder why they kill themselves at the rate they do.'

10 In very recent times there has been recognition on a national level that boys are in trouble. Last year Stephen O'Doherty, a State Liberal MP, chaired the then Government's Inquiry into Boys' Education, which identified the very real problems with the current generation of boys and recommended a strategy for gender equity in education. The inquiry was the result of direct concern about boys, from parents, educators and health workers.

11 'How to fix boys is the hottest current issue in education today,' O'Doherty told the *Herald* ...

12 In his introduction to *Boys in Schools*, the author of *Manhood*, Steve Biddulph, writes: 'We have to counter the signals sent to boys (from society, the media, from some women who hate men and some men who hate themselves) that being male is somehow intrinsically dirty, dangerous and inferior. Many boys now get this rejected feeling from all sides—overstretched or neglectful parents, stressed-out teachers, lingerie ads, soft-porn rock videos and from some girls.'

13 So what has happened to boys? Have they suddenly become pathological? Was maleness ever thus? Has twenty years of feminism made us intolerant of boys and their boyishness, their high spirits, their bravado, risk-taking and aggression? Do we all too readily want to suppress (often with drugs) and control boys' natural boisterousness?

> *Best thing about being male:*
> Don't have to wear a top when swimming. Drive fast, die young.
> *Worst thing:*
> Can't express my deeper feelings without being ostracised. Drive fast, die young.
>
> Views of teenage boys in *Boys in Schools*.

14 What is clear is that the sensible advocates for boys are still pro-feminist. They realise that girls, however superior at school, still don't get within a bull's roar of men in the working world. They stress that the important girls' education strategies must remain.

15 'What are girls' greatest problems? Males and their attitudes,' said Fred Carosi, leading teacher at Canterbury Boys', and the driving force behind the school's successful anti-violence program. 'If you want to fix up girls' problems, you have to fix up the boys.'

16 Fletcher agrees. 'What has changed is our complacency about boys' behaviours and attitudes. We are also recognising that we don't know much about boys. This is not the same as discovering that boys are oppressed, like girls, but it does mean noticing how poorly schools are serving boys.'

17 Boys' troubles are also linked to our notions of masculinity—that men are supposed to attain power, dominance, strength and physical prowess, and suppress shows of emotion, love and any interest in culture.

18 Schools, argues [Rollo] Browne, [who is co-editor of *Boys in Schools*,] can play a vital part in challenging and reshaping boys' understanding and experience of masculinity.

19 It's not easy. Schools still run on the dominant male model, where often the favourite role-model is the muscle-bound sports teacher, and the positions of authority are almost always male.

20 'A lot of teachers control classes with bullying and abuse, so kids can see hundreds of times that as adults we get what we want by controlling the behaviour of others,' Browne said ...

21 'As long as the boys' behaviours are seen simply as problems—violent boys, disruptive boys—then the programs developed to "fix" them will be policing operations,' Fletcher said.

22 'Unless we truly want our schools to become prisons with more and more discipline for boys, we will have to link the values we wish to teach with valuing the boys themselves.'

Sydney Morning Herald,
19 August 1995

listening

first date DISASTER

Melina Marchetta
Looking for Alibrandi

When girls and boys get together, the chemistry is not always perfect!

BETWEEN THE LINES

novel excerpt

Your teacher will read the synopsis and excerpt.

See the Appendix for guidelines on listening tasks before you attempt these questions and activities.

In this excerpt, Josie's mother has allowed her to go on her first date with Jacob Coote, but Josie has also persuaded Jacob to meet her mother beforehand. Josie spends a good deal of time on her appearance, and a good deal of time telling her mother about Jacob, especially the fact that he is a school captain.

The teacher will read an excerpt starting on page 120 with 'The doorbell rang and Mama raised her eyebrows and smiled' and ending on page 124 with 'I thought seriously of writing to *The Guinness Book of Records.*'

8.1 Jacob wears:
  a old jeans, a jumper with holes, an ear-ring and he hasn't shaved
  b old jeans, a jumper with holes in the sleeves, an ear-ring and stubble on his face
  c old black torn clothing and an ear-ring
  d old jeans, a jumper with holes, an ear-ring and trendy designer stubble.

8.2 Jacob has 'done it on purpose' probably because he:
  a always wears old clothes
  b resents having to meet Josie's mother
  c enjoys shocking people
  d is dressed to ride a motor bike.

8.3 The word closest in meaning to 'perplexed' is:
  a disappointed
  b shocked
  c bewildered
  d angry.

8.4 Josie turns away so her mother can't see her face because Josie:
  a agrees with her mother
  b probably looks sad and disappointed
  c might be rude to her mother
  d was crying.

8.5 Josie mentions *Morons from Outer Space* because:
 a it is a real movie
 b Jacob would like a movie with this title
 c she's at her wit's end
 d she is suggesting Jacob is a moron.

8.6 The main issue causing the conflict is that:
 a Jacob wants to be himself and not be boring
 b Josie's mother expects unreasonable standards of dress
 c Josie is intelligent and Jacob is a moron
 d Josie and Jacob have different standards of dress for a first date.

8.7 Pretend you are Jacob and write ten or twelve lines expressing your point of view about this episode.

8.8 What makes this excerpt from the book interesting and entertaining? Make brief notes on characters, language and the situation before writing your final answer.

CAREERS

chapter 4

This chapter focuses on one aspect of your future—the job or career you may choose or, at least, dream about.

You will be examining:
- the language of a newspaper article
- graphs
- information reports
- a novel excerpt
- an advertisement
- an instruction
- interviews
- a poem.

Writing activities include:
- summaries
- a speech
- a diary entry
- a résumé
- job applications
- a report
- a pamphlet
- an advertisement
- a listening excercise for the class.

The activities in this chapter should help to develop your skills for interpreting and constructing texts related to work. At the end of this chapter you should also know a good deal more about the problems and possibilities of employment.

1 **GREAT EXPECTATIONS**
Jane Freeman
'Young dreams'
'Pass with frying colours'
Charles Dickens
Great Expectations

2 **SOME FACTS**
Labour force status and age—August 1997
Labour force participation rate, males and females—1982–97
Employed persons, occupation—August 1997

3 **OPTIONS**
TAFE NSW
The Right Choice

4 **DESPERATELY SEEKING…**
Australia Bank

5 **SUCCESS BY DEGREES**
University of Sydney
Courses and Careers Day 1998

6 **JOB ALERT**
'JobWatch'

7 **THE APPLICATION**
Lyndall Hough
Résumé preparation

8 **TOADS**
Philip Larkin
'Toads'

9 Listening

WORKWISE
Face the panel

1 great EXPECTATIONS

newspaper feature article

Jane Freeman
'Young dreams'

From the time we are small, we are asked what we would like to be when we grow up. The question suggests we can be anything we wish, but how realistic are dreams and wishes in today's competitive job market?

BETWEEN THE LINES

Read the newspaper feature article on pages 79–83 and then complete the following questions and activities.

1.1 The phrase 'career choices don't match labour market realities' (paragraph 1) means:
   a the options available don't match what people want
   b the careers people prefer are only available sometimes
   c the careers people want are not real
   d people only want careers when they can choose them.

1.2 The word 'disillusioned' (paragraph 2) means:
   a freed from false impressions
   b informed about prospects
   c suffering from an illusion
   d depressed about prospects.

> **1.3** Have your dictionary on hand at all times.

1.3 The 'fin-de-siècle adolescent' (paragraph 8) is one who:
   a has finished school with little ambition and needs a job
   b is a selfish, careless, indulgent and decadent youth
   c belongs to the last generation of the century
   d has fewer ambitions than those of previous generations.

1.4 List the points that Hugh Mackay makes (paragraphs 9–16) and discuss them around the class. Write ten or twelve lines expressing your view on these matters.

1.5 There are two groups of young people described by Professor Don Edgar and Dr Wendy Patten (paragraphs 17–26). What are the two groups? Explain the reasons for the differences between the groups.

> **1.6** Refer to the Appendix for a model of a bar graph.

1.6 An A.C. Nielsen study is mentioned in paragraph 28. Present the study's findings as a bar graph.

1.7 Don Edgar says 'young people's ambitions do not always reflect the realities they will face when their education is finished' (paragraph 33). List the evidence presented for this point of view.

1.8 Write multiple-choice questions about the meaning of the terms 'linear career progressions', 'flattened career hierarchies' and 'fluid workforce' (paragraph 44).

> **1.8** Refer to the Appendix for guidelines on writing multiple-choice questions.

1.9 Peter Dwyer believes the workplace has changed (paragraph 44) but young people:
  a have not changed their expectations
  b have changed their expectations
  c all believe they will have jobs in 2001
  d generally believe they will have jobs in 2001.

1.10 For each 'expert' quoted in the section How to Beat Unemployment, write one sentence that clearly expresses his or her main point.

YOUNG DREAMS

1 Some young people don't have ambitions; others have great expectations. But the experts worry that many career choices don't match labour market realities.
JANE FREEMAN reports.

2 'What do you want to be when you grow up?' We have all been asked that embarrassing question as kids, dutifully trotting out 'fireman, doctor, nurse, actress, ranger...' But many young people today may question the relevance of ambition. With youth unemployment at almost 30 per cent, you can understand them being disillusioned about their career prospects. What's the point of having an ambition?

3 It may be more important than ever, say educationalists and psychologists. It's just that young people may need more than one ambition—to be flexible.

4 Ambitions, dreams and goals play an essential part in safeguarding well-being. In a world where adolescents seem more beset by 'temptations' (drugs, unplanned parenthood, suicide), aspirations can keep them from being waylaid.

5 And Mark Latham, the Federal Opposition spokesman on employment and youth affairs, believes we want young people to be '10 to 20 per cent over-ambitious' because of the high level of youth unemployment.

6 'That amount of overstriving and ambition gives them a nice match of effort and high hopes for the future,' he says.

7 Today's young people stay at school longer (in the past twenty years, the Year 12 retention rate has doubled to 70 per cent); they leave home later and fewer have full-time jobs.

8 Some commentators have suggested that the fin-de-siècle adolescent has fewer ambitions that his or her predecessors.

9 In his book *Generations*, social researcher Hugh Mackay characterises youth today as the 'options generation'.

10 'Whether they are thinking about a course of study, a job, a sexual partner, a political party, a set of religious beliefs, or even whether they'll be home for dinner tonight, they have decided to remain as non-committal as possible for as long as possible,' he writes.

11 'They do not fear the future, or the further changes it may bring, but they know that change will come, so stability and predictability—even as goals—seem rather incongruous.'

12 In May, Mackay told the Australian Human Resources Institute conference in Sydney that young people had decided work was not as important to them as it was for their parents.

13 'It would be a mistake to assume that at a time of high unemployment, young people will be scrambling to accept whatever job is on offer,' he said.

14 'On the contrary, we will have to woo them because they have already decided that work is not going to be as important

to them as it was to their parents.

15 They are interested in keeping their options open, they are looking for greater flexibility in the work that is offered to them. They want to know, more than their parents did, what's in it for me?

16 'They do not expect that an employer will take them on and keep them on forever. They expect neither to give nor to be given loyalty in the workplace.'

17 Professor Don Edgar, the founding director of the Australian Institute of Family Studies, agrees that not all of the next generation of young people are willing to slog away at a job, accepting that getting somewhere and achieving anything requires consistent hard effort.

18 'A lot of kids are even growing up in a house where neither of their parents have had a job for a long time ... they don't know what work means, so we can hardly expect them to have ambitions,' he says.

19 'Even goals we used to take for granted, such as wanting to buy a house or a flat and get married and have a family, are not as important.'

TWO TRIBES

20 HOWEVER, there are also the studies that show some young people have lofty expectations, at least when it comes to university education and professional status.

21 A study by Melbourne University's Youth Research Centre of almost 2000 people who began TAFE and university courses in or after 1992 showed most retained high ambitions.

22 Sixty-six per cent wanted to go into professional or managerial occupations and 61 per cent actually expected to.

23 Dr Wendy Patten, the editor of the *Australian Journal for Career Development* and a lecturer in career guidance at Queensland University of Technology, says the explanation of this apparent contradiction is that young people in the 1990s are more varied.

24 'We still have a group of young people wanting that traditional future and a traditional job, whereas another group realise they are never going to have it and are making other plans,' she says.

25 'Some are bright and determined to make a future that is equal to their parents. Then there are others who believe having an ambition is too difficult.

26 'It all depends on their own experience, their school, their background. If they have parents in traditional careers they are likely to expect the same for themselves. But we now have adolescents living in homes where none of the adults have ever worked.'

FAVOURITE JOBS

27 WHEN you ask young people to cite their preferred career, their choices have often not changed all that much from the choices of young people a decade ago. In 1989, a national sample of schoolchildren aged fourteen by the Australian Council for Educational Research's Longitudinal Surveys of Australian Youth found that adolescents aspired to be school-teachers, tradespeople, small business owners, police or army personnel and office workers.

28 This month, a multimillion dollar A.C. Nielsen study of 5700 young Australians... released last week, found that the biggest groups of Australian girls wanted to be either a teacher or a performer (9 per cent) or a vet (6 per cent), while boys wanted to be athletes (9 per cent), lawyers (8 per cent) or doctors (6 per cent).

29 The priorities are different in regional areas. A study of Year 9 to Year 12 students in regional centres by RMIT's Centre for Workplace Culture Change found that young people were interested in trades, farming, professional employment such as medicine and law and working with people in teaching or care work. By Year 12, the most popular ambition was in a trade, followed by child care/teaching, creative, sports, hospitality, the defence forces/police, law/medicine and journalism.

30 Centre director Professor Anna Bodi says young people's ambitions are formed from work experience, watching and talking to people employed in the fields, parents, teachers and the media.

31 'For example, becoming a reporter or a lawyer often looks cool on television,' she says.

FAR FETCHED?

32 DON Edgar says broad ambitions, such as wanting to make money or having a job that is satisfying or working with people, can give young people a sense of purpose while still leaving their options open, so they are not stuck on pursuing

one particular goal in life which may not be open to them.

33 However, young people's ambitions do not always reflect the realities they will face when their education is finished.

34 A 1994 Australian National Opinion Polls (ANOP) survey found that Australian high school students were unrealistic in their career aspirations, with many seeking positions in university or jobs which will not be available.

35 Fifty-six per cent of students in Years 10 to 12 who were questioned aspired to jobs in professional occupations (which make up only 13 per cent of the labour force).

36 Sixty per cent of students surveyed wanted to go to university, but only 30 per cent of that year's HSC class in NSW gained a university place. ANOP found most students aspired to higher education for employment-related reasons, but their employment aspirations were 'significantly out of line with current occupations in the workforce.'

37 Twenty-two per cent of the workforce is in clerical positions, but only 3 per cent of senior high school students aspired to this kind of work on leaving school.

38 More recently, the National Centre for Vocational Education Research looked at statistics comparing university students' occupational plans with actual labour force statistics for 1996–97. It found 'major discrepancies' between students' aspirations and the current distribution of employment among occupational groups, especially for the professional and para-professional groups for which students' occupational aspirations far exceeded current employment levels.

39 However, the opposite was true (aspirations well under current employment levels) for occupations such as managers and administrators, clerks, salespersons, plant and machinery operators and drivers and labourers. The exception was tradespersons, where the planned level was not far from the actual level of employment.

40 Associate Professor Peter Dwyer, of the University of Melbourne's youth research centre, told the biennial conference of the Careers Education Association of Victoria late last year that the long-term aspirations of many TAFE and university-educated people in their twenties were at odds with labour market realities.

41 Even worse off were their peers who left school early to face unemployment, underemployment and continuing social change.

42 The centre followed these early school leavers for three years and found 'tremendous zigzags in their lives', moving in and out of jobs, in and out of the family home, breaking up with their parents, going back to school and even trying another job.

43 'It was a chaotic and depressing picture,' Dwyer said.

44 Dwyer said the workplace had changed in many ways—no linear career progressions, flattened career hierarchies, a more fluid workforce. Even worse, there may be no job waiting for these young people. The centre's 1992 study found that while 66 per cent of young people wanted to go into professional or managerial occupations, only 40 per cent of those who have completed their studies were in a career job down the track.

45 'When we ask them what they expect to be doing in 2001, the vast majority expect to have full-time careers and not be at risk of unemployment or casual labour,' he said. 'Yet the realities of the labour market suggest a different set of outcomes.'

A DIFFERENT WORLD

46 THE kinds of work available have also been revolutionised, largely by technology.

47 Mark Latham, author of *Civilising Global Capital* (Allen and Unwin), points out that whereas in the 1950s and 1960s young people could be employed with 'relatively simple and repetitious skills' in agriculture, manufacturing and office work, we now have seen the advent of knowledge-based technology (as well as service industries, such as restaurants, child care, tourism and household functions).

48 'For a significant proportion of the labour force, a successful working life now requires a range of adaptable skills with a lifetime commitment to learning and reskilling, he writes.

49 He believes young people do have a strong appreciation of new technologies and the new knowledge-based jobs, both of the skills needed and the job opportunities.

50 But Anna Bodi says that while young people have firm

opinions on what are the 'cool' jobs—and these include some of the 'new' occupations, such as IT jobs and marketing—they lack a clear idea of where those jobs are. They think vaguely of some city skyscraper.

51. 'Manufacturing is clearly not "cool"—students perceive it as "noisy, dirty and smelly"', she says.
52. 'Jobs are changing fast, and manufacturing is changing fast. There are all kinds of jobs for young people in sectors like that.
53. 'Young people need to be helped when it comes to making career choices, so they know what their options are and where the options will lead them.'

How to beat unemployment: education, skills and a stint at Maccas

54. WITH the recent surge in youth unemployment, the thoughts of parents and young people are inevitably turning to ways in which they can avoid the unemployment trap.
55. **Professor Helen Hughes, of the Centre of Independent Studies**, decries people who tell adolescents how tough it is out there and so kill their fledgling aspirations.
56. 'It's important that they know that although 8 per cent of the population is unemployed [overall], 92 per cent are employed,' she says. 'The important thing is that they stay at school until Year 12 and then get themselves some training.
57. 'It's the kids who are leaving when they are sixteen that are in that 30 per cent unemployed group. And by training, I don't mean formal training at university—there are all kinds of other options these days.'
58. **Associate Professor Peter Dwyer, of the University of Melbourne's youth research centre**, says young people preparing for the workforce of the next millennium need a high degree of flexibility and resilience. One way to cultivate that is combining study with part-time work (and perhaps making it all financially viable by living at home).
59. 'Employers are looking for people who are flexible, who have portable skills, who know how to blend and mix, and these young people are doing it at a perhaps unconscious level,' he says.
60. **Professor Don Edgar, the founding director of the Australian Institute of Family Studies**, argues that career counsellors should stop focusing on specific vocations and start to focus on the skills young people need to develop to survive in a changed working world.
61. 'It's misleading just to tell them they need a goal; instead they need to be developing a variety of diverse skills,' he says.
62. 'Even when you talk to people now about how they got where they are, it's not often that it is just having an ambition and then setting out to achieve it. People achieve their current position by taking up opportunities as they came along.'
63. **Career guidance lecturer Dr Wendy Patten** admits that her hobby horse is good vocational training.
64. 'Parents should be knocking on the door of the school and asking what that school is going to do to facilitate their child's career development,' she says.
65. This is crucial. Young people need a set of skills that will prepare them for lifelong learning and career development—knowledge of their strengths and weaknesses, areas they need to develop, awareness of the world of work, decision-making skills, career transition skills. They now predict that people will have around seven different careers in a lifetime.
66. **Employment consultant Jacquie Wise**, a career guidance pioneer for students and author of *Career Comeback* (Wise Ways), says young people have to start viewing their careers as projects needing careful management.
67. She says employers want the combination of qualifications and commonsense that comes from experience in part-time jobs and activities

that require initiative and commitment, perhaps being involved in community service.

68 'Visibility is credibility … you need to get a reputation for excellence and a CV that makes you look like an achiever,' Wise says.

69 'I don't think you have just one career goal; I'd like to see a more lateral approach which is more realistic as well. You have to be flexible, prepare to take other things along the way and perhaps reach your goal in a lateral way.

70 'But the other problem young people have is pushing themselves. They have been taught instant gratification, everything comes so easily, so they are very different from the generations who worked hard because nothing came easily.'

71 And talking of hard yakka, a recent report of the House of Representatives' Standing Committee on Employment, Education and Training, A Working Solution, recommends ambitious youngsters take on a stint at McDonald's because 'McDonald's training is so successful in developing positive work-related attitudes in young people that its employees are universally valued by other employers.'

72 **Julie Owen, the director of corporate relations for McDonald's**, says employers want young people with McDonald's experience because of their people skills, customer service, confidence, work ethic and team spirit.

73 Owen says young people need to be guided to where the jobs are. 'There are good management careers in companies like this and other parts of the retail and hospitality industries. But we don't think young people know where these jobs are,' she says.

74 **The Shadow Employment Minister, Mark Latham**, emphasises that, in the end, education is the key to unlocking the future. 'It's not easy, but the more they learn, the more they earn,' he says.

Sydney Morning Herald, 15 August 1998

'Pass with frying colours'

newspaper report

Work experience has become an important step in preparing for the workforce.

Pass with frying colours

1 THE Federal Government wants NSW to count work done at McDonald's towards the HSC.

2 The Victorian Government took the lead this year by deciding to give students official recognition for their job training as part of the Year 12 leaving certificate.

3 Federal Minister for Schools, Vocational Education and Training, Chris Ellison, said the Government was keen to expand the involvement of industry in schools.

4 A spokeswoman for the NSW Board of Studies said there were no plans to follow the Victorian example in NSW.

5 But NSW school education policy director Doctor Bryan Cowling said NSW should follow the Victorian example of counting part-time work, such as with McDonald's, towards the HSC.

Sun-Herald, 5 July 1998

BETWEEN THE LINES

> **1.11** A definition of 'satire' appears in the Key Terms section of the Appendix.

1.11 Explain how the cartoon at the beginning of the report is satirical and humorous.

1.12 The headline, 'Pass with frying colours', is an example of:
   a a simile
   b personification
   c a pun
   d alliteration.

> **1.12** Definitions of these words appear in the Key Terms section of the Appendix.

1.13 What does 'official recognition' (paragraph 2) mean? Write a definition that does not include either word.

> **1.14** A model of a formal letter appears in the Letters section of the Appendix.

1.14 Writing

Write a letter to the NSW Board of Studies expressing your viewpoint about counting work done at McDonald's towards the HSC. For example, do you think the skills learned at such work are relevant to the HSC, do you think that it would be merely useful publicity for McDonald's, or do you have another view?

---

novel excerpt

Charles Dickens
Great Expectations

The more things change, the more they stay the same.

When young Pip, the blacksmith's apprentice, discovers that a mysterious and anonymous person has bestowed a fortune on him, he travels to London for his education and to realise his 'great expectations'. He is placed in the care and guidance of Herbert Pocket, a young man of genteel breeding, who is also making his way in London. They have rooms in Barnard's Inn, a dilapidated lodging house. In this excerpt, over their first dinner together they discuss Herbert's career.

BETWEEN THE LINES

Read the novel excerpt on page 85 and then complete the following questions and activities.

1.15 In line 2, the word 'capitalist' means someone:
   a who takes a great deal of risk
   b with money to invest in business
   c who works in the city and insures ships
   d who makes money from shares.

(continued p. 86)

We were very gay and sociable, and I asked him, in the course of conversation, what he was? He replied, 'A capitalist—an Insurer of Ships.' I suppose he saw me glancing about the room in search of some tokens of Shipping, or capital, for he added, 'In the City'.

5   I had grand ideas of the wealth and importance of Insurers of Ships in the City, and I began to think with awe, of having laid a young Insurer on his back, blackened his enterprising eye, and cut his responsible head open. But, again, there came upon me, for my relief, that odd impression that Herbert Pocket would never be
10 very successful or rich.

'I shall not rest satisfied with merely employing my capital in insuring ships. I shall buy up some good Life Assurance shares, and cut into the Direction. I shall also do a little in the mining way. None of these things will interfere with my chartering a few
15 thousand tons on my own account. I think I shall trade,' said he, leaning back in his chair, 'to the East Indies, for silks, shawls, spices, dyes, drugs, and precious woods. It's an interesting trade.'

'And the profits are large?' said I.

'Tremendous!' said he.

20 I wavered again, and began to think here were greater expectations than my own.

'I think I shall trade, also,' said he, putting his thumbs in his waistcoat pockets, 'to the West Indies, for sugar, tobacco, and rum. Also to Ceylon, specially for elephants' tusks.'

25 'You will want a good many ships,' said I.

'A perfect fleet,' said he.

Quite overpowered by the magnificence of these transactions, I asked him where the ships he insured mostly traded to at present?

'I haven't begun insuring yet,' he replied. 'I am looking about
30 me.'

Somehow, that pursuit seemed more in keeping with Barnard's Inn. I said (in a tone of conviction), 'Ah-h!'

'Yes. I am in a counting-house, and looking about me.'

'Is a counting-house profitable?' I asked.

35 'To — do you mean to the young fellow who's in it?' he asked, in reply.

'Yes; to you.'

'Why, n-no: not to me.' He said this with the air of one carefully reckoning up and striking a balance. 'Not directly profitable. That
40 is, it doesn't pay me anything, and I have to—keep myself.'

This certainly had not a profitable appearance, and I shook my head as if I would imply that it would be difficult to lay by much accumulative capital from such a source of income.

'But the thing is,' said Herbert Pocket, 'that you look about you.
45 *That's* the grand thing. You are in a counting-house, you know, and you look about you.'

It struck me as a singular implication that you couldn't be out of a counting-house, you know, and look about you; but I silently deferred to his experience.

> Pip realises that they have met before as children and had a fight, during which Pip blackened Herbert's eye.

1.16 Herbert appears to be:
  a an experienced young man
  b an ambitious young man
  c a realistic planner
  d an unrealistic dreamer.

1.17 Explain the reasons for your answer to 1.15.

1.18 Pip could best be described as:
  a inexperienced but intuitive
  b innocent and ignorant
  c gullible and silly
  d critical and inquisitive.

1.19 Explain the reasons for your answer to 1.17.

1.20 Research the meaning of 'counting-house'.

> **1.20** A definition of 'tone' appears in the Key Terms section of the Appendix.

1.21 Compare Herbert's attitude that it's a 'grand thing' to 'look about you' with the advice given by the experts in the How to Beat Unemployment section of the newspaper article 'Young dreams' (pp. 82–3).

Before writing your answer, make notes on the following aspects of each piece.
- In what ways are the messages of each piece the same? In what ways are they different?
- Is the purpose of each piece different? For example, the writer of the second piece is creating an impression of a character, the writers of the other piece are giving advice.
- How different is the language used in each piece? Are there differences just because the novel was written in the nineteenth century or are there differences because of the purposes of the writers? Think about the tone of the writing in order to answer this question. The experts quoted in the newspaper article sound definite, while Herbert sounds uncertain. What words, phrases and expressions give these impressions?

Write about a page.

2 some FACTS

It is always useful to be well-informed about a situation. The Commonwealth Bureau of Statistics regularly publishes useful statistics on a wide range of topics, including Australian youth. Here are some samples.

Labour force status and age—August 1997

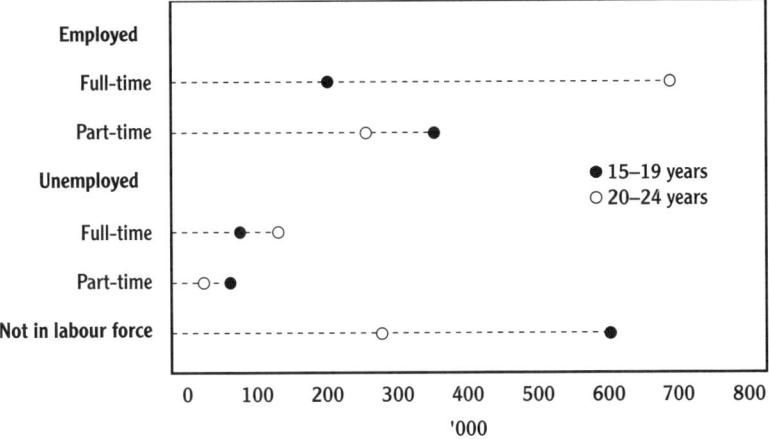

dot graph

AGPS (Commonwealth Information Service)

Labour force participation rate, males and females—1982-97

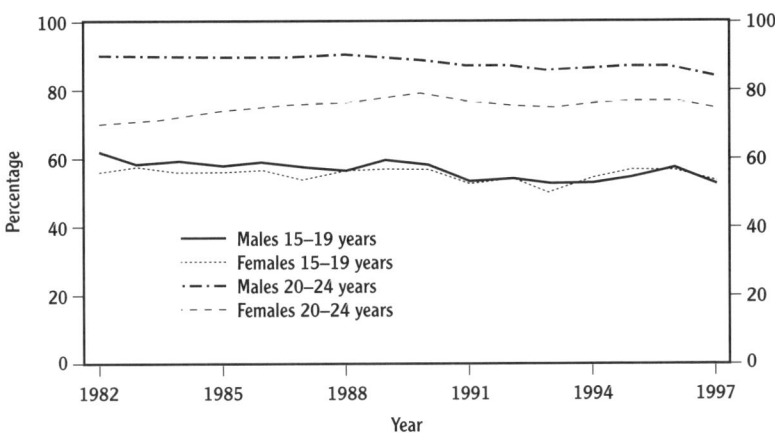

line graph

AGPS (Commonwealth Information Service)

Employed persons, occupation—August 1997

information grid

Occupation	15–19 years (%)	20–24 years (%)	25 years and over (%)
Managers and administrators	0.4	1.6	9.0
Professionals	1.3	11.7	19.8
Associate professionals	3.0	7.6	11.7
Tradespersons and related workers	12.9	17.2	13.1
Advanced clerical and service workers	1.5	5.0	4.8
Intermediate clerical, sales and service workers	15.0	22.0	15.8
Intermediate production and transport workers	7.8	7.8	9.5
Elementary clerical, sales and service workers	38.4	15.0	7.0
Labourers and related workers	19.6	12.0	9.4
All occupations	**100.0**	**100.0**	**100.0**
	'000	'000	'000
All occupations	**553.4**	**941.9**	**6820.2**

AGPS (Commonwealth Information Service)

CAREERS

BETWEEN THE LINES

Questions and activities 2.1 to 2.3 require you to copy out the paragraphs and then fill in the blanks by studying the information supplied in the graphs and grid. Some answers may only require one word, while others may require a phrase or sentence.

2.1 When people looking for work register with a job agency, they indicate whether they want full-time or part-time work. The Commonwealth Bureau of Statistics, which makes these graphs, therefore knows whether or not unemployed people are looking for full-time or part-time jobs.

2.1 Using the dot graph, complete the following cloze exercise.
There are only about _____ thousand 15–19 year olds in full-time work, probably because _____ .
   This may also explain why this age group is employed in more _____ jobs than the 20–24 year olds. Nonetheless, among unemployed 15–19 year olds, more were looking for _____ work than _____ work.

2.2 Using the line graph, complete the following cloze exercise.
In the 15–19 years age group, participation rates for males and females have _____ during 1982–97. In the 20–24 years age group, labour force participation rates are _____ for males than for _____ , probably because _____ . However, the gap between men and women in the 20–24 years age group has _____ over time. For males aged 20–24 years, the labour force participation rate has _____ during 1982–97, but for women, it has _____ .

2.3 Using the information grid, complete the following cloze exercise.
The highest percentage (_____) of people aged 15–19 years worked as _____ in 1997 and nearly 20 per cent worked as _____ . This is probably because _____ .
   The highest proportion of people aged 20–24 years work as _____ and the lowest proportion of people aged over 25 years work as _____ .

3. OPTIONS

information report

TAFE NSW
The Right Choice

TAFE stands for Technical and Further Education. TAFE Colleges offering the courses outlined in *The Right Choice* train thousands of people every year in a wide variety of courses, ranging from Accounting to Visual Arts.

BUILDING AND CONSTRUCTION

BUILDING

BUILDING CONSTRUCTION
QUALIFICATION: TAFE STATEMENT
COURSE NO: 2152
This course teaches the procedures and practices for domestic and commercial building construction. The course may be used as a bridging course for entry into other building courses, or as a means of obtaining recognition of prior learning for building qualifications.

BUILDING STUDIES
QUALIFICATION: DIPLOMA AQF
COURSE NO: 2183
This course teaches you building and management skills and how to include social, environmental and legal aspects into building projects. When you finish the course you will have the qualifications for a Builder's Licence. Some of the technical areas in the course are building construction, quantities and estimating, management, surveying, building safety and advanced building computing. On completion you can apply for Building Advanced Diploma 2184 or advanced standing in building courses at several universities.

Career Opportunities

- Builder
- Bricklayer
- Residential Draftsperson

BRICKLAYING

BRICKLAYING—TRADE
QUALIFICATION: CERTIFICATE III AQF
COURSE NO: 2160
This course is for apprentices working in the bricklaying trade. It teaches you how to lay and bond bricks and similar building blocks for domestic, commercial and public buildings, and how to construct ornamental panels, feature walls, arches and columns. You also will learn how to prepare and maintain brickwork. On completion you can apply for Building Studies, Residential Certificate IV 2182.

BRICKLAYING—SKILLS
QUALIFICATION: CERTIFICATE I AQF
COURSE NO: 2170
This course teaches you the skills you need to work in bricklaying and about changes in technology, wage structures and working conditions. You also learn how to communicate with customers, fellow workers, suppliers, supervisors and employers. On completion you can apply for advanced standing in Bricklaying—Trade Certificate III 2160.

BRICK AND SEGMENTAL PAVING
QUALIFICATION: TAFE STATEMENT
COURSE NO: 2171
This is an introductory course for people employed or seeking employment as paviours.

ARCHITECTURAL STUDIES

ARCHITECTURAL TECHNOLOGY
QUALIFICATION: CERTIFICATE IV AQF
COURSE NO: 2186
This course is for people who want to learn architectural drafting skills for the residential construction industry. It trains you in how to present and document projects using both manual and computer aided drafting (CAD) techniques. The course covers construction methods and how to include social and environmental aspects into residential construction projects. Some of the technical areas covered in the course are construction methods, presentation, building materials, architectural technology, and CAD and related computing skills. This course replaces the first half of Architectural Drafting Associate Diploma 5195. When you finish this course you can do Architectural Technology Diploma 2187.

VOXPOP

'I've got an apprenticeship, so I study and work at the same time. I like the hands-on experience here. If you want to work for yourself in a trade, I think you're better off at TAFE. After I get my Builder's Licence, I can do another course to help me start my own bricklaying business.'

Trent Hale, 20, Bricklaying

CAREERS 89

BETWEEN THE LINES

3.1 Study the way the information is arranged on the page. Make notes about the headings, the point size (that is, the size of the text), the use of boxes to divide the information, and the links between the pieces of information and the VOX POP section. Organise your notes and write ten to twelve lines about the layout of the page.

3.2 The information in each box is divided into the following sections: the name of the course, what you learn in the course and the qualifications you gain. Identify these sections of information in each box. Write a similar description for a job that you are employed to do, or that a parent or a friend is employed to do.

3.3 Which course or courses might Trent Hale be enrolled in?

3.4 What do you think 'VOX POP' means? What is the value of the VOX POP section?

3.5 The language used in this information report is:
   a factual and technical
   b metaphoric and colourful
   c clear and simple
   d suitable for everyone.

3.6 Write three or four lines justifying your answer to 3.5.

4 desperately SEEKING...

advertisement

Australia Bank

Perhaps you want to start working right away and learn on the job. Keep an eye on the employment sections of newspapers, both local and state. You may see something like the advertisement on page 91.

BETWEEN THE LINES

4.1 Refer to the Appendix for guidelines on analysing visual texts and for a definition of 'tone' (see Key Terms section).

Study the advertisement on page 91 and then complete the following activities.

4.1 Comment on the design and content of this advertisement. Study the font, point size, layout, information, tone, repetition and general effectiveness. Write about ten to twelve lines.

4.2 Design an advertisement for a part-time worker at:
  a a salon for pampered pets
  OR
  b a zoo
  OR
  c Paddy's Markets.

University of Sydney
Courses and Careers Day 1998

information report

When you leave school you have many options. Attending university is one of them. Perhaps you will achieve 'success by degrees'. It may seem difficult to earn a place in a university, but the following excerpt from a university booklet shows you that universities really do want you and they put a good deal of effort and money into attracting your attention. One university recently used an aeroplane to fly its message up and down the coast during the summer holidays!

Success by Degrees

ADAM SPENCER
TV AND RADIO HOST Arts graduate

At Courses and Careers Day Adam will be hosting the great debate 'Student days are the best days of your life'

You'll find Sydney graduates in almost every imaginable career from Prime Minister to Rock Star. A degree from Sydney can lead in unexpected directions, and with the future gazers telling us that by 2015 half of the workforce will be doing jobs that don't even exist yet, perhaps that is just as well. Here three Sydney graduates talk about how Sydney Uni helped them.

A First Class Honours degree in pure mathematics sounds like pretty serious stuff—for a funny man.

But comedian Adam Spencer—best known as Triple J's drive show presenter, stand-up comic, and regular 'Good News Week' guest—does have a serious side. Viewers of ABC TV's science show, 'Quantum', which Adam has hosted since the beginning of the year, have seen that a comedian can do science with outstanding success. Adam says there is no reason why a fascination with the mathematical and scientific world should preclude anyone from a career in comedy—or vice versa. In fact, Sydney University is the perfect training ground for both.

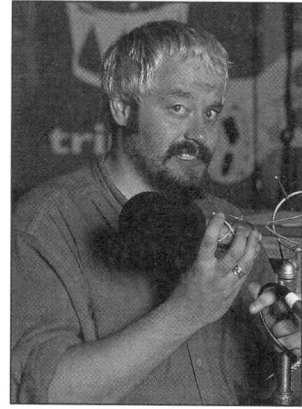

It was at Sydney University, while Adam was studying for a combined degree in mathematics and law that the extracurricular seductions of the Debating Club and Theatresports caught him in their net. He did well in both, winning the Australasian Universities Debating Championships twice and being runner-up in three World Championships. As MC for Theatresports, Adam found that he was funnier than most of the competitors, and appreciative audiences of his stand-up comedy routines at nearby Harold Park Hotel agreed.

In 1996, halfway through a PhD in pure mathematics, Adam won Triple J's Raw Comedy Competition. This resulted in occasional radio appearances, and a brief apprenticeship on the midnight to dawn shift before graduating to the 3–6 p.m. drive show, The Departure Lounge.

When the ABC approached twenty-nine-year-old Adam to host 'Quantum' late last year, wanting to broaden the reach of the program, the bulk of the viewing audience was over fifty-five. Six months into his stewardship, the sixteen to twenty-four-year-old audience has doubled.

LUCY CREAGH
ARCHITECT

The opportunity to work as a research assistant to the Faculty of Architecture's Professor Lawrence Nield, designer of the Multi-Use Arena at the Homebush Bay Olympic site, gave Lucy Creagh her entrée to the high-profile job which would make her the envy of many of her colleagues.

Lucy gained valuable experience with Professor Nield which was to pave the way for an appointment to the Government Architect Design Directorate, set up to develop the detail of the master plan for the Olympic site.

'The master plan is like a snapshot of the whole site taken from the air,' says Lucy. 'It was our job to zoom in on details like paving, design and placement of street furniture, lighting, colour selection, and signage. My role was to write the briefs, engage consultants and organise the site ready for its first public event—the 1998 Easter Show.'

After graduating with a BArch (Hons) in 1992, her first job was in the Government Architect's Office's Research Unit, working on urban design projects including the George Street upgrade, in collaboration with the Sydney City Council.

'While I've worked primarily on urban design,' Lucy says, 'I've had experience of everything from domestic scale work to commercial, and I've worked on some interesting and unusual projects. When the opportunities came I took them, without thinking too much about where I was going or whether they would be good for my career.'

TIM FREEDMAN
MUSICIAN Arts Graduate

Tim Freedman's is the first name you will see on the surfboard located just inside the Manning Bar. It was inscribed there when, in 1984 as an Arts/Law undergraduate, Tim and his band of the time, You're a Damn Good Detective, Detective, won a Sydney University band competition.

That was when Tim, now lead singer of The Whitlams, 'got serious' about his music. He'd been playing piano and singing since he was a kid, and it was while he was at Sydney University that he had the chance to do gigs on campus and in pubs around Camperdown and Newtown.

It was at one of these Newtown pubs that Tim got together with the other 'between bands' musicians who were to form The Whitlams in 1992. Billy Heckenberg (drums), Cottco Lovett (bass), Ben Fink (guitar), Chris Abrahams (keyboard) and Tim (vocals) cut their first CD 'Introducing the Whitlams' for Phantom Records a year later, to be followed by 'Undeniably the Whitlams' and 'Eternal Nightcap', which has sold 100 000 copies in Australia alone.

Why the name? 'We just thought it was a funny name,' says Tim. 'It refers to an idealistic period of Australian history, and we're fans of Gough and Margaret. I've had a chat with Gough and he thinks it's a good name. We're his favourite band and he wishes us well.'

BETWEEN THE LINES

5.1 The headline 'success by degrees' implies:
  a success is something that is achieved slowly
  b success can be achieved through university degrees
  c you cannot be successful without a degree
  d both a and b.

5.2 Do you think this information is organised and presented effectively? In your answer discuss three features of the layout and explain whether or not you think the content is interesting.

5.3 Decide whether the following statements are true or false. Write a sentence to justify your choice in each case.
  a At university your activities are dictated by the course you are studying.
  b Comedy has become more important than science for Adam Spencer.
  c Lucy Creagh's job requires more skills than knowledge of architectural urban, domestic and commercial design.
  d Tim Freedman has a sense of humour and can recognise an opportunity.

5.4 Writing
'Student days are the best days of your life' is the debate topic mentioned in the report. Imagine you are debating this topic. Choose which side you would prefer to argue and write a speech of about 600 words. You could take either a humorous or a serious approach.

> **5.4** Refer to the Appendix for guidelines on writing and delivering speeches.

6 job ALERT

information report

'JobWatch'

Keep informed. Read about the job market and find out where the opportunities may be.

BETWEEN THE LINES

Read the information report on pages 95 and 96 and then complete the following questions and activities.

6.1 In groups, select one of the suggested jobs, or choose another from the employment section of your local paper and research it carefully.

6.2 Having collected all possible information, write a letter or a diary entry about one of the following:

a an acting workshop with your favourite soapie star

OR

b your experiences as a nanny working overseas

OR

c your new business started through NEIS

OR

d fruit picking in the Goulburn Valley (or anywhere else)

OR

e your first week or two at a job you found advertised in the local newspaper.

JobWatch

Playing the part

Any young aspiring actors out there can start to hone their skills with a training workshop run by the Australian Theatre for Young People.

Australia's oldest youth theatre company offers a number of courses that give teenagers the opportunity to work alongside some of the country's top theatre actors.

This winter, the ATYP offers Acting For The Camera with Grant Bowler (from 'Medivac' and 'Blue Heelers') and Go Go classes with Annette Evans from Kip Hefner's 'Wild World of Women'.

The company also presents classes that include acting, performance building, circus, directing, design and singing.

Holiday workshops will run between 6 July and 17 July with term workshops from 27 July until 20 September.

Classes are held in Parramatta, Chatswood and The Wharf Theatre in the city.

Nanny academy

One way to work your way around the world is to become a nanny with the skills sought by any parent in need of a child carer.

The Dial-an-Angel service has been established for thirty years and since 1996 has helped more than 200 students into nannying careers.

The academy offers a twelve-week training course that teaches students everything from caring for a newborn baby to making playdough and balancing the family budget.

Full-time study requires attendance three days a week in the classroom, with two days spent in a private family home for practical experience.

For those unable to move to Canberra to study, the academy also offers open learning, which allows students to complete the course at their own pace and is aimed at the employed who wish to enter the child-care field.

The total cost of the twelve-week full-time course is $1500; the open learning option costs $1200. Various payment methods are available.

On your own

Working for yourself can be one of the most rewarding things, especially in a business you started yourself.

The Eastern Suburbs Business Enterprise Centre has an accredited Small Business Management Course for people who are registered with Centrelink as unemployed and have a business idea.

The course is part of the Federal Government's New Enterprise Incentive Scheme (NEIS) and encourages unemployed people to start their own small business.

People who take part in NEIS are also entitled to a payment of an allowance for up to twelve months equivalent to Newstart, and advice and assistance from business mentors in the first twelve months of operation.

The course takes six weeks with the next one starting on 6 October.

Applications close on 11 September.

Take your pick

Seasonal work picking, packing and grading fruit is a great way to see some of the more remote areas of NSW and is almost always available.

The hills around Coffs Harbour abound with banana plantations but from September to January every year blueberries are harvested.

Like many coastal seasonal areas job opportunities arise at certain times of the year for fruit pickers and packers.

Experienced pickers are mostly required in Coffs Harbour, but from September to November it is possible for inexperienced pickers to get a start.

There is also shed work available, packing and grading the fruit.

There are normally about 200 places offered.

In Cowra, September heralds the start of the asparagus harvest and up to 400 cutters are needed.

The harvest begins in mid-September and lasts for about ten weeks depending on conditions.

The work is constant and physically demanding, with cutters working outdoors for six hours a day.

Cutters are paid by the amount of asparagus they cut with different rates for first- and second-grade asparagus.

Daily Telegraph, 4 July 1998 and 29 August 1998

7  the APPLICATION

instruction

Lyndall Hough
Résumé preparation

Applications are important. They are the first point of contact between you and a possible employer so they need to make a good impression.

Résumé preparation

Before you prepare your résumé, collect examples from other people that you know. Look at the way they have ordered the information and the general design and layout. Choose one that you like and model yours on that, adding your own personal touches.

Presentation: Use a computer or typewriter; most people do. A handwritten résumé, unless specifically asked for, looks unprofessional. Some prospective employers ask for handwritten applications to see if you can spell and are literate. If that is the case, make sure that your spelling is correct and your handwriting is neat and legible. Always use good-quality paper.

Design and layout: Organise your résumé so that it is easy to read. Use headings that clearly indicate the subject underneath, for example Name, Address, Age, Previous Work History and Experience, Educational History, and Qualifications.
Use short paragraphs in which the necessary information is clear.

Length: Most companies prefer two pages, but you could use up to five.

Method of presentation: Some people prefer to write their details in chronological order; that is, in the order they occurred. Other people prefer to show how they can do the job advertised, demonstrating their skills and achievements and how they fit the job criteria.
Include the material that you think is important to show that you can do the job.

Covering letter: The covering letter is what the future employer reads first. It should answer the requirements in the advertisement. That means you should be able to show you can meet the essential criteria for the job. Take each requirement and answer it in a short paragraph. Indicate why you are suitable for the job.

References: Give the names, addresses and phone numbers of your referees. Don't include your references, as the person opening the letter may lose them. If you wish to include them, use good photocopies. The employer may phone the referees for further information.

Lyndall Hough, *In Fact*

BETWEEN THE LINES

> **7.1** A definition of 'imperative verbs' appears in the Key Terms section of the Appendix.

7.1 Identify the following features in the instruction:
  a a clear title indicating the subject matter
  b a list of the materials needed
  c a clear series of steps to follow
  d the use of imperative verbs
  e the use of simple language
  f short, clear sentences.

> **7.2** Refer to the Job Applications section of the Appendix for guidelines on preparing a résumé and covering letter.

7.2 Writing

Using the résumé preparation instruction, prepare a résumé and a covering letter to apply for one of the jobs mentioned in this chapter. If you wish to apply for a different job, attach a copy of the advertisement, or a job description you have written yourself, to your résumé and letter.

7.3 Writing

In groups, prepare a pamphlet of information and advice about careers, job hunting and applications that would be useful for people of your age.

Use the information in this chapter, the experiences of your friends and your own general knowledge. Your pamphlet should be attractive visually and written in simple language. You should use illustrations, including photographs and diagrams, as well as written material.

Peer assess the pamphlets when they are completed. Your careers advisor could also assess them and perhaps they could be handed out on careers night.

8 TOADS

poem

Philip Larkin
'Toads'

We all profess to want to work; work is good for us; it pays the bills; it gives us purpose and self-assurance, not to mention *in*surance. But here is another view, and we would be less than honest if we did not admit that sometimes this is exactly how we feel.

BETWEEN THE LINES

8.1 Study the poem on page 100 and then use the clues on page 101 to work out which words from the poem fit into the grid provided on page 101. You will need to copy the grid. Five letters are already in the grid to help you start.

8.1 Have your dictionary on hand at all times.

8.2 Copy out the following short passage about the poem, replacing the numbered space with the most suitable alternative provided for that number.

The poem 'Toads' expresses a [**8.3**] idea about work. The poet is irritated by the way work ruins his freedom; he compares work to a toad to express his disgust and uses words such as [**8.4**] to convey the strength of his feelings. The effort of working to pay a few bills [**8.5**]. He wishes he could live like other folk do, that is [**8.6**], and he observes that they don't end as paupers.

He knows, however, that he doesn't have the courage to reject his job: he is too [**8.7**]. He also seems to be realistic, as evidenced by the line [**8.8**]. He explains that something 'toad-like / Squats in me too' and this 'something' probably makes him fearful of [**8.9**]. The images that suggest his fear are [**8.10**].

The final stanza suggests that it is [**8.11**] when you have both conservative and rebellious character traits.

8.3 **a** ridiculous
    b whimsical
    c serious
    d hilarious

8.4 Include at least two examples.

8.5 **a** matches what you gain
    b spoils every day of the week
    c makes him ill all week
    d is out of proportion

8.6 **a** lazily
    b luckily
    c cleverly
    d miserably

8.7 **a** dreamy
    b conservative
    c radical
    d silly

8.8 Add the appropriate line.

8.9 **a** taking risks
    b stealing the money
    c being irresponsible
    d talking too much

8.10 Add two appropriate examples.

8.11 **a** spiritual
    b difficult to change
    c hard to be happy
    d admirable

'Toads'
by Philip Larkin

Why should I let the toad *work*
Squat on my life?
Can't I use my wit as a pitchfork
And drive the brute off?

5 Six days of the week it soils
With its sickening poison—
Just for paying a few bills!
That's out of proportion.

Lots of folk live on their wits:
10 Lecturers, lispers,
Losels, loblolly-men, louts—
They don't end as paupers.

Lots of folk live up lanes
With a fire in a bucket;
15 Eat windfalls and tinned sardines—
They seem to like it.

Their nippers have got bare feet,
Their unspeakable wives
Are skinny as whippets—and yet
20 No one actually *starves*.

Ah, were I courageous enough
To shout *Stuff your pension!*
But I know, all too well, that's the stuff
That dreams are made on:

25 For something sufficiently toad-like
Squats in me too;
Its hunkers are heavy as hard luck,
And cold as snow,

And will never allow me to blarney
30 My way to getting
The fame and the girl and the money
All at one sitting.

I don't say, one bodies the other
One's spiritual truth;
35 But I do say it's hard to lose either,
When you have both.

John and Dorothy Colmer (eds), *Mainly Modern*

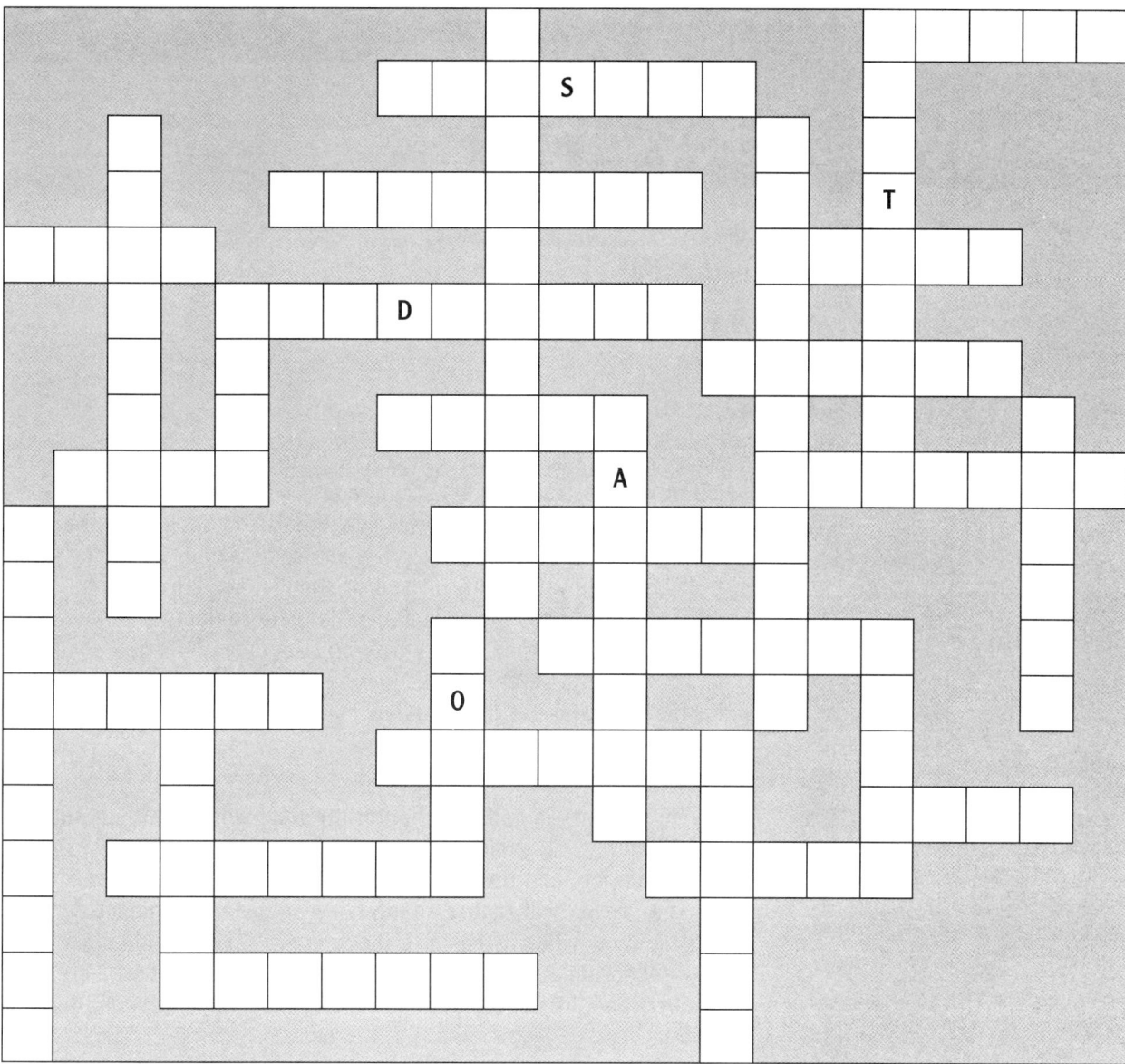

People (4)
Labour (4)
Cleverness (4)
Good fortune (4)
Accounts (5)
Beast (5)
Dirties (5)
Pathways (5)
Frog-like amphibians (5)
Young ruffians (5)
Ne'er-do-wells (6)
Images in sleep (6)
Harmful substance (6)
Emaciated (6)
Crouches (6)

Allowance (7)
Poor people (7)
Thpeakers! (7)
Smooth talk (7)
Calf muscles (7)
Kids (7)
Dies from hunger (7)
Good rabbit hunters (8)
Baby pilchards (8)
Instructors (9)
Implement (9)
Good fortune (9)
Ratio (10)
Doctors' helpers (11)
Objectionable (11)

The numbers indicate the number of letters in each word you need to find.

listening

9 WORKWISE

interviews

Face the panel

Direct experience is the best teacher.

BETWEEN THE LINES

Refer to the Appendix for guidelines on listening tasks before you attempt either of these activities.

Refer to the Interviews section of the Appendix for guidelines on job interviews.

9.1 Have someone in your class interview a student who has a part-time job or who has recently left school and is working. Tape the interview. The interview should cover how the person applied for the job, what happened at the job interview and some details about the job itself. Is it enjoyable, difficult and/or stimulating? What are the problems? What are the advantages? Is there contact with other people? What are they like? and so on. The taped interview should be about five to seven minutes long. Prepare seven or eight questions for the class and use the interview as a listening exercise.

OR

Divide the class in half. One half of the class will prepare questions to interview a job applicant for Australia Bank (see pages 90–1), or another job, and the other half will prepare to be interviewed.

The teacher will choose an interviewing panel and one or two interviewees. While listening to the interviews, you should make notes about the quality of questioning (that is, the content and manner) and the demeanour and tone of the interviewers and the interviewees.

Write a brief report, recommending one of the interviewees for the job and supporting your recommendation with evidence.

INDEPENDENCE

chapter 5

Everyone eventually needs to develop independence from home, school and parents. Independence is attractive, challenging and scary, all at the same time.

In this chapter you will be reading and viewing a range of material, including:
- novel excerpts
- a short story
- newspaper feature articles.

You will be asked to write:
- a newspaper report
- a diary entry
- a language analysis
- a piece of creative writing
- a speech
- a segment for a radio program
- a listening test.

1 **ONE WAY OUT**
Steve Dow
'Why children run away from home'

2 **WAR**
Guy Edwards

3 **BREADWINNER**
Thomas Hardy
Tess of the D'Urbervilles

4 **OUTCAST**
Henry Fielding
Tom Jones

5 **GAY RIGHTS**
Cameron Sharp
Hamilton High School Speech

6 **IDENTITY CRISIS**
Michelle Gunn
'Youth suffers identity crisis as rites of passage blur'

7 **POLITICS**
Stephanie Peatling
'PolitiKids'

8 Listening

ON YOUR OWN
School's out

1 one way OUT

| newspaper feature article | **Steve Dow**
'Why children run away from home'

Do all young people want independence or is it sometimes the only way out of seemingly impossible situations? |

BETWEEN THE LINES

Read the newspaper feature article on pages 105–7 and then complete the following questions and activities.

1.1 In paragraph 1, 'social security support' refers to:
  a help and shelter from friends
  b shelter provided by organisations
  c hand-outs from various people
  d money paid by the government.

1.2 In the second sentence of paragraph 5, 'vice versa' means:
  a this is the one possible, correct explanation
  b the child's story is favoured over the parent's
  c there is no danger if the parent's story is right
  d there is no danger if the child's story is right.

1.3 'But there's another, more complex story about Calib' (paragraph 9) suggests:
  a we cannot accept the known facts at face value
  b each story is biased in favour of a particular view
  c there is additional, complicated information
  d both the stories are fictional and unbelievable.

1.4 Steve Dow includes the paragraph about Calib playing the piano (paragraph 12) because:
  a Calib has a great deal of talent that is being wasted
  b Calib is not really talented because he cannot read music
  c the only tune Calib can play is 'Stairway to Heaven'
  d Calib wastes time playing music. He should be working.

> **1.5** Definitions of 'jargon', 'imagery' and 'pun' appear in the Key Terms section of the Appendix.

> **1.5** 'The Wall' refers to a notorious spot in Darlinghurst, Sydney, where young men sell their bodies for sex.

1.5 In paragraph 13, the expression 'the Wall' is an example of:
  a crude language
  b jargon
  c imagery
  d a pun.

1.6 Find out what a 'custody order' (paragraph 28) is.

1.7 In paragraph 5, Steve Dow writes that there is 'usually anguish on both sides', that is both parent and child experience anguish. Do you think his article illustrates this successfully? Why or why not? Write about twelve lines.

Why children run away from home

1 Some have no shelter. None have a permanent home. And, unless they have been kicked out or can prove abuse, there is often no social security support.

2 About 21 000 Australians aged under eighteen are homeless, according to the Centre for Youth Affairs, Research and Development at RMIT. At best, they have only temporary shelter. Fewer than half get government benefits: the Federal Government's Centrelink job search office says 9164 Australians under eighteen get the independent homeless support rate, a category of the youth training allowance, which pays a maximum of $240 a fortnight.

3 In November, the Government will introduce a 'hotline' that parents of teenage runaways can call to air their views on whether or not their child should be eligible for the allowance.

4 A spokeswoman for the Minister for Social Security, Senator Jocelyn Newman, says some parents believe it is 'too easy for their kids to claim they're homeless' and thus collect the allowance. But critics argue that it is a budget cut in disguise: a way of tightening the already tough criteria for homeless children seeking social security. Youth workers believe the initiative signals that the Government automatically assumes children are lying when they say they cannot live at home.

5 When a teenager runs away, there is, of course, usually anguish on both sides, and both parent and runaway will have their own version of events. Perhaps the danger is that, when a parent's story is always favoured over that of a child, or vice versa, the chasm of pain between them will deepen.

CALIB'S STORY

6 WHICH story about Calib* do you want to hear? The story of the sixteen-year-old who ran away from his Bayswater home at fourteen because, he says, he couldn't handle the daily arguments with his mother? Two years later, he can barely recall what the arguments were about. Smoking in his room, he suggests, was one point of difference.

7 Perhaps you might agree with Calib when he admits that leaving was a 'stupid thing to do'. The arguments were over little things. 'They seemed to be bad then because they were happening to me every day.' He never intended to leave for good. A few weeks after leaving home, Calib left school after telling his form coordinator to 'go jump' when asked to remove his nose ring and ear rings.

8 But there's another, more complex story about Calib.

9 Consider that Calib was failing at school because he has attention deficit disorder. Consider that, at age ten, he was taken to a psychiatrist when his mum and dad busted up. 'We used to get along OK until they broke up.' Consider that Calib has had to come to terms with being gay.

10 And consider that he tried living at home with his mother and little brother again. It didn't work. Again, there were arguments every day.

11 Calib sits, now, at the piano in (yet another) temporary home with a family who provides care for runaways. He plays Stairway to Heaven. He can also play tenor tuba and clarinet, and has started learning drums because there is a drum kit in this house. He can't read music. He plays by ear.

12 There hasn't been much time to practise. Shortly after running away, he met a slightly older teenager who convinced him to go to Sydney. 'He got a hotel room and walked me up past "the Wall". Somehow he convinced me (when he said) "oh no, we've got no money left".' For a couple of months, Calib sold his body to the gutter crawlers of Kings Cross. 'It was disgusting. But I liked it for the money.' He earned $200 a night.

13. A Salvation Army worker in Sydney tried to get Calib on to the independent homeless support allowance instead. Calib even filled out an application form. No luck. 'I couldn't get the allowance because I left home, I wasn't kicked out.'
14. He was telephoning his grandmother in Melbourne most days. She convinced him to come home at Christmas, 1996. A succession of refuges and emergency accommodation followed. He inhaled solvents, slit his wrists, and, later, took an overdose of 20 Rohypnol tablets. 'Just too much stress and stuff,' he says.
15. 'Having no one help you is the worst thing. I didn't go and ask for help. It's easier for me when people come up to me and ask if I want any help.' That's what the Salvation Army did.
16. On the day we meet, Calib has a job interview lined up at a hamburger store. Ultimately, he would like to get into hairdressing, or maybe play in a band.
17. 'I'm getting there, slowly,' he says, with short, friendly smiles. 'Just going along with what happens. Just hope it works out.' His voice trails off ...

MARILYN'S STORY

18. MARILYN says her daughter was only ever hit once. In late 1995, she confronted her youngest child, Emma*, then twelve, about whether a packet of cigarettes was hers.
19. Emma barricaded herself in her bedroom for the entire weekend. Late on Sunday, her father smashed down the door. As Emma tried to escape via a window, her father hit her.
20. "And that's the only time, ever,' says Marilyn. 'He will have to live with that for the rest of his life ... he can't forgive himself ... but why should he have to feel like that when it was virtually her fault?'
21. Emma ran to a neighbour, who reported Emma's father for hitting her to the Department of Health (now Human Services).
22. After staying with a friend for a couple of days, Emma returned home. In late 1996, she ran away again, this time for two weeks, because, says Marilyn, of an argument over going to a disco.
23. In early 1997, Marilyn started getting telephone calls that Emma wasn't turning up to school. It turned out she had been truanting with a friend. That March, she went missing for several days. Marilyn and her husband notified the department. Emma was found, but her parents were asked to sign a notice of protection application, placing Emma in foster care.
24. Marilyn says they had no choice but to sign the order to secure their daughter's safety. 'It was terrible,' she says. 'It implied we can't or have not looked after our child, or we're going to physically harm our child.'
25. In the time since, Emma has been in a foster home, from which she has run away, has been found by police, overdosed on heroin, and has had a pregnancy terminated.
26. This week, Emma turned fifteen. She is living temporarily in a lock-up care facility run by the Human Services Department for her own safety, after being found in the city, after taking heroin.
27. Marilyn fears that, when Emma's custody order (keeping her in the department's care) expires in July, she will refuse to return home. She says her daughter boasts of getting independent homeless support.
28. Marilyn vacillates when asked whether her daughter will have a home to which she can return. At first, she says she is 'not prepared at this stage to have (Emma) back in the house' because of her heroin use. But then she says: 'We want her home. Definitely. But can you imagine, after the lifestyle she's been living, to be living here? It would be horrific for all of us. She'd probably rob us. She'd probably still keep going on with this heroin thing.'
29. Marilyn finds the Emma of today difficult to reconcile with the girl growing up, who did well at school up until Year 8, who used to smile sweetly and say: 'Good night, love you, sweet dreams.'
30. Marilyn thinks some of the problems have been caused by a lack of self-esteem. Emma was conscious from the age of ten of being much taller than other girls. There was also the company Emma kept and the fact she did not like discipline.
31. 'Can you imagine how it makes me feel as a mother?'

she says. 'I have just felt lately that I've not been a good mother.' Marilyn's lips start quivering and tears well up in her eyes.

32 'We don't understand why she's doing this.'

33 Marilyn is taking antidepressants. She makes regular attempts to see her daughter.

Sometimes, Emma wants to see her. At other times, the welfare workers tell her mother: 'No, sorry.'

Age, 25 May 1998

* Names of the young people in these stories have been changed because they are subject to court orders.

2 WAR

Guy Edwards

letter

A very different type of independence has been the lot of many young people through the centuries. Read this letter, which was written by a soldier to his younger brother in Australia towards the end of World War I.

BETWEEN THE LINES

2.1 Read and write out the following comment on the letter (see page 108), filling in the spaces as you go.

This letter is probably typical of many such letters written during the war. The writer, Guy, seems typical too, of young _____ overseas. He is fascinated by what he sees and in awe of the _____ of London compared to Sydney. He compares Sydney to _____ .

His enthusiasm for London is evidenced by the phrases _____ [find three examples].

He also includes some observations about social conditions. For example, he mentions the _____ [find three examples].

Like many people of the time, he is shy of using direct expressions. In the opening sentence he uses the euphemism _____ [quote it], which really refers to _____ . In the second last sentence he also indirectly refers to _____ .

Guy's punctuation and sentence structure are not always correct. For example, _____ [find one example of incorrect punctuation and one of incorrect sentence structure]. However, the letter presents a vivid impression of his experience, and his excitement is conveyed to the reader through the jumble of details. An example of this use of detail is _____ [quote a phrase or sentence].

2.1 As you fill in the blanks, remember to make sure that your writing makes sense without having to change any of the given words and sentences.

2.1 A definition of 'euphemism' appears in the Key Terms section of the Appendix.

This letter is clearly written in a different time period. Three words or phrases that show this are _____, _____ and _____ .

Interestingly, he finishes the letter by advising his young brother not to _____ because _____ (use your own words).

> **2.2 Refer to the Appendix for guidelines on newspaper reports.**

2.2 Writing

You are an Australian war correspondent in London during World War I. Use the information from the letter and your responses to activity 2.1 (above) to write a newspaper report for your Australian newspaper about life in London. Remember to give the report an interesting headline. Write about 300 to 400 words.

No. 3 Battery
3rd Division
active service abroad

18 March 1918

My dear Doug,
Just a note before we go over to France, we hop across on Tuesday and get straight to business. We had our leave in London seven days and had a great time. It is worth seeing, the size of it is wonderful. There are miles and miles of houses and shops, hotels, theatres, factories. Sydney is like a currant in a bun to it. The bus service there would be just into your hands — seats on top. There are a terrible lot of women working at all sorts of employment. The Australian girls would do well to see them and take the tip from them. We went to three or four good theatres and tried all the top notch restaurants and hotels. Food is very dear but the English people are far from starving, as there is plenty of employment for young and old. There are thousands of pretty girls in London, it's hard to realise where they all come from. I never saw so many. You see a good few in Australia but here they are in hundreds.

Three-quarters of the male population here in the streets are in khaki and those who are not are small weedy and old or too young.

Eric, Arthur and I are all together still and hope to keep so all the time. We saw the Tower of London and the Tower Bridge, the Law Courts, St Pauls Cathedral, the Houses of Commons and Lords and Westminster Abbey and the London Waxworks and the Art Gallery and take it from me they are worth seeing and opened our eyes I can tell you. Well old chap good night and good luck.
I hope to come back some day but if I don't it's just what they call doing your bit. This is a rotten life and for goodness sake don't enlist whatever you do, as it's not worthwhile and there is too much waste of time and red tape and humbugging.

Love from

Guy

BETWEEN THE LINES

BREADWINNER

Thomas Hardy
Tess of the D'Urbervilles

novel excerpt

The following novel excerpt indicates that independence was often difficult and dangerous for young people in the nineteenth century. The teenage children were often the breadwinners for their whole family.

Tess Durbeyfield is the daughter of a poor villager, who finds out that he is descended from the ancient and noble family of D'Urberville. The Durbeyfields decide to send Tess, their eldest child, to work for the family who have taken the D'Urberville name. The son, Alec, is already attracted to Tess, and Mrs Durbeyfield has a romantic notion that he will marry Tess and make her a lady. She takes care that Tess looks particularly beautiful the day she leaves for her new position.

1   So the girls and their mother all walked together, a child on each side of Tess, holding her hand, and looking at her meditatively from time to time, as at one who was about to do great things; her mother just behind with the smallest; the group forming a picture of honest beauty flanked by innocence, and backed by simple-souled vanity. They followed the way till they reached the beginning of the ascent …

2   'Bide here a bit, and the cart will soon come, no doubt,' said Mrs Durbeyfield. 'Yes, I see it yonder!' …

3   Her mother and the children thereupon decided to go no farther, and bidding them a hasty good-bye Tess bent her steps up the hill.

4   They saw her white shape draw near to the spring-cart, on which her box was already placed. But before she had quite reached it another vehicle shot out from a clump of trees on the summit, came round the bend of the road there, passed the luggage-cart, and halted beside Tess, who looked up as if in great surprise.

5   Her mother perceived, for the first time, that the second vehicle was not a humble conveyance like the first, but a spick-and-span gig or dog-cart, highly varnished and equipped. The driver was a young man of three- or four-and-twenty, with a cigar between his teeth; wearing a dandy cap, drab jacket, breeches of the same hue, white neckcloth, stick-up collar, and brown driving-gloves—in short, he was the handsome, horsey young buck who had visited Joan a week or two before to get her answer about Tess.*

6   Mrs Durbeyfield clapped her hands like a child. Then she looked down, then stared again. Could she be deceived as to the meaning of this?

* Alec D'Urberville.

Prince was the family carthorse and their only means of earning a living. He was killed in an accident on the road, and Tess believes she is responsible.

7   'Is dat the gentleman-kinsman who'll make Sissy a lady?' asked the youngest child.

8   Meanwhile the muslined form of Tess could be seen standing still, undecided, beside this turn-out, whose owner was talking to her. Her seeming indecision was, in fact, more than indecision: it was misgiving. She would have preferred the humble cart. The young man dismounted, and appeared to urge her to ascend. She turned her face down the hill to her relatives, and regarded the little group. Something seemed to quicken her to a determination: possibly the thought that she had killed Prince. She suddenly stepped up; he mounted beside her, and immediately whipped on the horse. In a moment they had passed the slow cart with the box, and disappeared behind the shoulder of the hill.

9   Directly Tess was out of sight, and the interest of the matter as a drama was at an end, the little ones' eyes filled with tears. The youngest child said, 'I wish poor, poor Tess wasn't gone away to be a lady!' and, lowering the corners of his lips, burst out crying. The new point of view was infectious, and the next child did likewise, and then the next, till the whole three of them wailed loud.

10 There were tears also in Joan Durbeyfield's eyes as she turned to go home. But by the time she had got back to the village she was passively trusting to the favour of accident. However, in bed that night she sighed, and her husband asked her what was the matter.

11 'Oh, I don't know exactly,' she said. 'I was thinking that perhaps it would ha' been better if Tess had not gone.'

12 'Oughtn't ye to have thought of that before?'

13 'Well, 'tis a chance for the maid—Still, if 'twere the doing again, I wouldn't let her go till I had found out whether the gentleman is really a good-hearted young man and choice over her as his kinswoman.'

14 'Yes, you ought, perhaps, to ha' done that,' snored Sir John.

15 Joan Durbeyfield always managed to find consolation somewhere: 'Well, as one of the genuine stock, she ought to make her way with 'en, if she plays her trump card aright. And if he don't marry her afore he will after. For that he's all afire wi' love for her any eye can see.'

16 'What's her trump card? Her d'Urberville blood, you mean?'

17 'No, stupid; her face—as 'twas mine.'

BETWEEN THE LINES

3.1 The children look at Tess 'as at one who was about to do great things' (paragraph 1). This suggests that the children:

a thought Tess looked beautiful
b were in awe of Tess
c were intimidated by Tess
d loved Tess and would miss her.

3.2 In your own words, describe the 'picture' mentioned in the first sentence. Compare your description with other group members.

3.3 Work out the meanings of the archaic expressions 'bide', 'yonder' and 'bent her steps'. Write three or four lines explaining the effect they have on the writing.

3.4 Research paragraph 5. For example, find out what a 'gig' and a 'dog-cart' are and what a 'dandy cap' and a 'drab jacket' look like.

3.5 The description of Alec suggests he is a:
   a considerate young man who spares no expense
   b flashy young man trying to impress Tess
   c neat and tidy young man
   d handsome young man who admires Tess.

3.6 'It was misgiving' (paragraph 8) means that Tess:
   a was apprehensive about Alec's offer
   b did not want to give Alec anything
   c had changed her mind
   d was in a state of indecision.

3.7 Explain the meaning of 'Directly Tess was out of sight, and the interest of the matter as a drama was at an end…' (paragraph 9).

3.8 Joan Durbeyfield was 'passively trusting to the favour of accident' (paragraph 10) means that she was:
   a trusting that Alec would have an accident
   b hoping that things would turn out luckily for Tess
   c hoping Tess would not have any accidents
   d ignoring the situation because it was out of her hands.

3.9 Examine the comments made by 'Sir John' in this excerpt (paragraphs 12, 14 and 16). What do they tell you about his attitude to his family? Give reasons for your answer.

3.10 Explain Joan Durbeyfield's feelings about Tess's new position. What does she hope for? Does she have doubts about the outcome? Why or why not? How do you know? Write about ten to twelve lines.

3.11 Tess's 'trump card' is her:
   a beauty
   b D'Urberville blood
   c inheritance
   d dowry.

3.12 Explain the irony of Mrs Durbeyfield's final statement.

3.13 Writing
Write the scene described in paragraph 8 from Tess's point of view, as though she is writing a diary entry. Express her feelings about her parents, brothers and sisters and the reasons for her decision to go with Alec.

> **3.12** A definition of 'irony' appears in the Key Terms section of the Appendix.

4 OUTCAST

novel excerpt

Henry Fielding
Tom Jones

Independence can be thrust upon you. The eighteenth-century novel *Tom Jones* is the story of an illegitimate boy who is adopted by the wealthy and kind Mr Allworthy. However, Tom is hated by Mr Allworthy's nephew, who eventually influences his uncle to throw Tom out of the house. To add to his miseries, Tom has fallen in love with Sophia Weston, the neighbour's daughter.

BETWEEN THE LINES

Read the novel excerpt on page 113 and then complete the following questions and activities.

4.1 Use your dictionary to look up unfamiliar words.

4.1 Decide whether the following statements are true or false.
   a In paragraph 1, 'whithersoever he should order them' means wherever he should order them to be sent.
   b Tom is so distracted that he walks a mile without noticing where he is going.
   c The description of Tom's behaviour in paragraph 3 shows how miserable Tom is.
   d 'His grief now took another turn and discharged itself in a gentler way' (paragraph 4) probably means Tom was crying.
   e Paragraph 4 indicates that Tom is now ready to plot his revenge.
   f 'Rent his heart asunder' (paragraph 5) indicates that Tom's heart is breaking at the thought of leaving Sophia.

4.2 Which of the following statements is closer to the meaning of the second sentence in paragraph 5?
   a Tom is miserable about leaving Sophia and would like her to come with him to share his poverty but he's not sure she would agree.
   OR
   b Tom is miserable about leaving Sophia, but even more so to think of reducing her to poverty. Even if he asked her to come because he wanted her so much, he is not certain she would.

4.3 Which of the following statements is closer to the meaning of the third sentence in paragraph 5?
   a Tom decided to leave Sophia, not pursue her, because he really loved her and he had consideration for Mr Allworthy's feelings.
   OR
   b Tom's despair and Mr Allworthy's resentment at Tom's behaviour overcame his burning desire to possess Sophia.

4.4 In groups, work out the meaning of paragraph 6 and rewrite it in your own words. You will need a dictionary and you will need to understand the imagery.

4.5 Do you think that the writer is laughing at Tom? Write about eight lines and support your opinion with evidence.

4.6 The four items so far in this chapter are all written in different styles. Write about a page explaining the purpose of each piece and how this is related to the features of the writing.

> 4.4 A definition of 'imagery' appears in the Key Terms section of the Appendix.

> 4.4 Refer to the Appendix for guidelines on style.

1. Jones was commanded to leave the house immediately and told that his clothes and everything else should be sent to him whithersoever he should order them.

2. He accordingly set out and walked above a mile, not regarding, and indeed scarce knowing, whither he went. At length, a little brook obstructing his passage, he threw himself down by the side of it, nor could he help muttering with some little indignation, 'Sure my father will not deny me this place to rest in?'

3. Here he presently fell into the most violent agonies, tearing his hair from his head and using most other actions which generally accompany fits of madness, rage, and despair.

4. When he had in this manner vented the first emotions of passion, he began to come a little to himself. His grief now took another turn and discharged itself in a gentler way till he became, at last, cool enough to reason with his passion and to consider what steps were proper to be taken in his deplorable condition.

5. And now the great doubt was how to act with regard to Sophia. The thoughts of leaving her almost rent his heart asunder, but the consideration of reducing her to ruin and beggary still racked him, if possible, more; and if the violent desire of possessing her person could have induced him to listen one moment to this alternative, still he was by no means certain of her resolution to indulge his wishes at so high an expense. The resentment of Mr Allworthy and the injury he must do to his quiet argued strongly against this latter; and lastly, the apparent impossibility of his success, even if he would sacrifice all these considerations to it, came to his assistance; and thus honour at last, backed with despair, with gratitude to his benefactor, and with real love to his mistress, got the better of burning desire, and he resolved rather to quit Sophia than to pursue her to her ruin.

6. It is difficult for any who have not felt it to conceive the glowing warmth which filled his breast on the first contemplation of this victory over his passion. Pride flattered him so agreeably that his mind perhaps enjoyed perfect happiness, but this was only momentary; Sophia soon returned to his imagination and allayed the joy of his triumph with no less bitter pangs than a good-natured general must feel when he surveys the bleeding heaps at the price of whose blood he hath purchased his laurels; for thousands of tender ideas lay murdered before our conqueror.

5 gay RIGHTS

short story

Cameron Sharp
Hamilton High School Speech

Independence need not be simply a matter of learning to survive on your own. It often involves facing up to personal issues and difficulties and accepting them.

This short story illustrates how independence can be challenging and confronting.

In September 1991 I was invited to speak at the Hamilton High School seventy-fifth Anniversary Reunion as the 'representative' of the students of the seventies. Hamilton is a small town of ten thousand inhabitants in deepest western Victoria, surrounded by a mostly prosperous and almost inevitably conservative farming community. This is the speech and its story.

Hi. I'm going to try and keep this short. It's hot and Friday and when I went to Hamilton High School, which was from 1974 to 1979, the last thing, and I mean the very last thing, I wanted to be doing on a hot Friday afternoon was sitting in this assembly hall, listening to a bunch of old boys and girls going on about how good it was in their day. Mind you, I don't know where you'd run off to have a smoke before getting the bus home, because they seem to have built on just about all the good hiding spots.

[A ripple of laughter from the back rows.]

That'll give you some idea that I was not always one to stay out of trouble. As a quick aside, there was a time when I pissed off one of my teachers and got chucked out of my English class. All I'd done was ask for some Durex—you know, sticky tape—to finish off some presentation but I found myself in the hall. For once I really didn't know what I'd done wrong. The vice-principal believed me, to his credit, and went up to find out what had happened. I discovered a long time later that in England, where my teacher came from, Durex is the name they use for condoms.

[They liked me. I'd said 'pissed off' in front of the assembled dignitaries, talked about frangers and known what it was like to be on the wrong side of the law. Little did they suspect.]

And just a bit more history. In the seventies anyone who wanted to have a 'pash' would do it behind 'D' block at lunchtime.

[Quite a lot of muttering.]

Good. It's nice to know that some things don't change.

When your principal asked me to speak here today, he asked me to think about the school motto, 'I shall attain', what it meant to me, how Hamilton High School helped prepare me for when I left and what I have done since then. 'I shall attain.' I'll come back to that.

Briefly, I've been around the world a couple of times. I never ended up going to uni because I liked travelling and didn't see the point. I have worked as a typist, a street musician, a paper recycler, a baker and a truck driver, but most recently I have come back from Stockholm, Sweden's capital, where I have been helping to organise the Annual World Conference of the International Lesbian and Gay Association.

[I left space for a reaction. It was a good idea. There were close to one thousand people crammed into the hall. Seven hundred and fifty students, a hundred teachers, present and past, and the rest were locals who may well have had many of their 'best days' behind 'D' block. There is nothing to compare with a thousand jaws slamming onto a wooden floor, a thousand people whispering 'Did you hear that? Did he just say...?' One elderly 'old boy' was fanning himself on stage behind me and gasping for breath. I tapped the microphone.]

I've got a bit more to say, actually, so as soon as you're ready, I'll carry on.

You may realise that being a young gay man here at Hamilton High School in the seventies was not a lot of fun. I would guess, from your reaction a second ago, that things probably haven't changed one heck of a lot. Which is a pity.

[My knees were shaking. There was an almost silence as a thousand people leaned forward to listen. I'd done it. Almost. Now I just had to get out of there alive.]

When I left here at the age of seventeen, I'd had six years of being terrified that, every time someone shouted 'poofter' across the yard, they had found out about me and that I was about to get my head bashed in (and possibly the rest of me).

If things haven't changed here in twelve years, then the world out there has. The world that is waiting for all of you when you finish here, whenever that may be, is the most amazing and fantastic place. And it doesn't matter if you don't get beyond Melbourne, or if you end up in Timbuktu. All that you need to know is that it will be very different and sometimes a bit scary. The time you spend here, and what you do with it, will sort out a lot about how you get on with life out there in the wider world.

'I shall attain.' Well, I didn't need to attain anything. I had it from the start, and what I had was being different.

Not just a bit different, but different in a way that made my life really miserable because of all the people during my time at school who would pick on anyone who wasn't just like them. It's sad, but I think they wasted six years here *not* attaining a bit of patience, a bit of respect for other people, a bit of common humanity. Not such a huge concept. It basically means that you try and get on with people.

So there I was. Different and surrounded by a bunch of people who thought they were my friends. People who did not in fact have any idea about who I really was, because I didn't know whom I could trust, and so I kept it hidden inside me until I could find people whom I could trust. In the end I never told anyone but ended up hanging out in a small and pretty exciting group made up of all the other 'odd' kids. The thing we had in common was that we were all different in some way and that we knew there was safety in numbers.

Now, that was pretty frustrating, having to stay hidden, but I got on with school and did fairly well. Until everyone started going out with each other—Leanne and Steven, Andrea and Ricky. I could tell you about a few girlfriends your science teacher Mr Steer had, as we were in the same year here.

[Heads turned.]

But I won't.

[A little laughter welling up here and there. My knees had locked and I dared not move them.]

Try and imagine how hard it would be not to be able to fall in love when everyone around you is. Even the kids in my group of outsiders were falling in love but I couldn't. Because it was dangerous. Not just physically but because of the threat that I would be kicked out of home, ridiculed, hated, despised and a lot of other things besides. I was lucky, because I never learnt to hate. But I was bitter and angry and I took out that anger on everyone around me.

By the end of form five, as it was called in my time, I had been threatened with expulsion three times. These were not the sort of visits to the vice-principal's office that could be laughed off, like a condom joke. I was an angry and frustrated and mixed-up young man who did not respect his teachers and made it very, very obvious. I could do the work—that wasn't the problem. But in those days there were no school counsellors, no gay men or lesbians who you knew about or could talk to, nothing in the library to tell me about homosexuality—nothing good, that is. Hamilton was a very small town. In short, it was a bloody lonely time.

And I don't think it's a lot better now.

I got my HSC and left Hamilton and I have only been back to visit my mum and dad at Christmas every other year or so. Because once I left, I found that there was this world outside Hamilton that opened up to me. As well as all the sort of people who'd yell 'poofter' at you across the yard or the street or wherever, there were all these other people who accepted me for who I really was.

So, to be honest with you, I don't know what I attained here at high school. Perhaps Hamilton High taught me that I had to protest to survive. I have certainly been doing that since I left. I've chained myself to bulldozers on the Franklin River; I've marched against nuclear weapons; I worked for Greenpeace for four years.

Perhaps, from my difficult times here, I attained an insight into a world of people who do not have such an easy time. Since leaving, I have been involved in a number of HIV/AIDS support groups and have worked as a counsellor. Along with that, I have also been involved in social justice and human rights organisations.

Perhaps what I attained here was the need to question everything that was presented to me as part of the norm, because it wasn't a world I recognised easily, even as a boy.

What *you* attain is going to be as individual as you want it to be.

I know it's hot and a Friday but I'd like to add that it's actually great for me to be here. After all I've said, that might sound a bit odd but I came here today, more nervous than you can possibly imagine, for one reason. Years ago I sat in this hall, a very despairing young man who thought he was completely alone. If someone had stood up here on this stage and said to me, 'Hey it's okay. Just hang in there, it'll all be okay,' then I would have been saved more pain and anguish than I care to remember.

I am here today because I *am* sitting out there in the hall. I could be your best mate, someone in the choir, the girl or boy who is sitting behind you in class. I could be anybody. And what you do with that idea will say a lot about what you are attaining here. If you leave this hall today and head out into that wider world unable to cope with the idea of there being people who are different to you, if you continue to shout 'poofter' and bash up kids because they're not as tough as you, then you're not attaining anything.

But if you can accept that people have a right to respect, to common decency and that thing I called humanity—well I think you get the point.

'I shall attain.' What I hope is that you strive to attain lives that let other people, in all their variety, teach you just how great it can be to be challenged. About how enjoyable it can be to think about things you've never thought about before. I hope there'll be a million opportunities to respect the variety that goes into making up our community and that you don't waste any of them. Because it's not about whether or not someone is a poofter or a leso.

It's about people. It's about you, me, him, her, them. Us.

Good luck.

[I couldn't move. I stood there, and there was what seemed like a very long silence before the place exploded into applause. Up the back they were stomping their feet, whistling. A number of students rose to their feet, some in groups or rows, others in pairs, and a few brave individuals by themselves. I was ready to cry.

Coming out in the place I feared the most was the bravest thing I think I have ever done.]

Next morning, shopping in the single main street, I was accosted by a woman whose choice of clothing reflected her undying support for the Australian Wool Corporation. She was smiling.

'My children haven't stopped talking about you. Well done. It's just what this place needed, a good shot up the backside. And about time. You see them leave, the young ones, because they don't think people here will understand them, and they're probably right, so they go to the cities.' She took a breath. 'But my kids have so many questions. I don't know what to say. I don't know what the answers are.'

I didn't know either. If there are any. But her kids were asking questions. That, at least, was a start.

Andy Griffiths (ed.), *Blasters: Risks and Challenges*

BETWEEN THE LINES

5.1 What were the problems the writer faced as a gay student in his high school? How have the attitudes of students changed since he was at school? Write about ten to twelve lines.

5.2 At various intervals in the story, Cameron Sharp writes some comments in brackets. What is the purpose of this?

5.3 Refer to the Appendix for guidelines on speeches.

5.3 Write down at least two reasons why this may be considered a good speech.

5.4 Using the speech in this short story as a model, write down all the features that could serve as guidelines for speech writing. Organise them into a logical order and compare your notes with those of other students.

5.5 This is a short story that contains a speech. Using the Appendix guidelines on narrative structure, analyse how well this story conforms to the usual narrative structure.

5.6 Writing

Prepare a speech on the issue of independence. You may choose a topic such as your first day at your first job, an incident from childhood when you needed to be independent or your first girlfriend or boyfriend.

Present your speeches to the class for peer assessment.

5.7 Writing
Group activity

It is Youth Week and you and several other school students have been asked to present a short segment on Triple J Radio. The topic is 'independence'. Your segment could take the form of a conversation, a play script, a selection of comments from various people, extracts from various writings and so on.

Prepare your segment, tape it and play it to the class for peer assessment.

6 IDENTITY crisis

newspaper feature article

Michelle Gunn
'Youth suffers identity crisis as rites of passage blur'

Independence can also bring frustrations.

Youth suffers identity crisis as rites of passage blur

1. It used to be that everyone knew when a young person became an adult. Enrolling to vote, enlisting for war, getting married or being handed a silver key with 21 inscribed in the middle—the signposts were all there.

2. But the old rites of passage have lost their meaning. The lines between adolescence and maturity have become blurred.

3. 'My parents are pretty hypocritical,' says Adam Pascoe, sixteen. 'They say if you act like an adult, we will treat you like one. But when it comes to asking if I can go out or something, all that is forgotten.'

4. And says Simon Henry, also sixteen. 'They encourage you to be responsible and everything, but then they also want to treat you like a boy for the rest of your life.'

5. It sounds like typical teenage angst. And in many ways it is. But young people today face a peculiar set of challenges.

6. A shrinking youth labour market; increasing numbers of young people staying on at school and university; delayed marriage and child rearing; a dramatic rise in part-time work; high levels of youth unemployment; and the trend towards earlier sexual activity all redefine the way the years fifteen to twenty-four are lived.

7. The director of Melbourne University's Youth Research Centre, Associate Professor Johanna Wyn, explains that the process of becoming an adult has been extended.

8. 'Once, achieving a livelihood was possible by getting a full-time job on leaving school at sixteen or seventeen, and young people were able to live independently of their parents in affordable accommodation by the time they were twenty,' she says.

9. 'This has become unheard of. Instead, getting full-time work is delayed until after a period of education and training; and living independently is very difficult.' The issue has been highlighted in recent months by changes in government policies which tie the level of unemployment benefits, and Austudy payment for young people to their parents' income.

10. 'The Government seems determined to redefine adulthood for young people whenever it suits them,' says a spokeswoman for the Australian Youth Policy and Action Coalition, Ms Michelle Giglio.

11. The great majority of fifteen to nineteen-year-olds live with their parents. But the past few decades have seen a huge increase in the proportion of twenty to twenty-four-year-olds also living at home, particularly among women, with a jump from 29.3 per cent in 1983 to 37.5 per cent in 1994.

12. The trend is partly explained by more people staying at school and going on to university.

13. Adam Pascoe, Simon Henry, Michael Gore, Amanda Quayle and Trish Noble all intend to go to university. And all see themselves living at home with their parents until after they graduate.

14. For many who persist with independent living, times can be tough. A quarter of single fifteen to twenty-four-year-olds live in poverty, almost double the rate for the general population, and recent figures indicate that young people make up more than a third of the nation's homeless.

15. This is linked to rising unemployment and the shrinkage of the full-time youth labour market. The number of teenage males in full-time work fell by more than a third in the years 1989–95, from 271 300 to 165 500 and whereas half of all school leavers went straight into full-time jobs in 1985, a decade later the figure had fallen to just 28 per cent.

Weekend Australian,
26–27 April 1997

BETWEEN THE LINES

Study the article, discuss it in your group and then complete the activities.

6.1 What are two events, mentioned in paragraph 1, that may be called 'rites of passage'?

6.2 'Young people today face a peculiar set of challenges' (paragraph 5). List three of these challenges.

6.3 What evidence is presented at the end of the article that the youth labour market is shrinking?

6.4 'The great majority of fifteen to nineteen-year-olds live with their parents' (paragraph 11). Suggest one reason why this is the trend and explain how this fact is related to the idea expressed in the headline?

> **6.5** Refer to the Appendix for guidelines on the structure of multiple-choice questions.

6.5 In groups, prepare multiple-choice questions on the following:
  a the meaning of the word 'hypocritical' (paragraph 3)
  b the meaning of 'typical teenage angst' (paragraph 5)
  c the meaning of 'tie the level of unemployment benefits, and Austudy payments for young people to their parents' income' (paragraph 9)
  d the implication of the comment 'the Government seems determined to redefine adulthood for young people whenever it suits them' (paragraph 10).

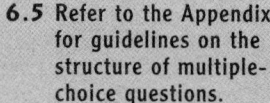

7 POLITICS

newspaper feature article

Stephanie Peatling
'PolitiKids'

During 1998, many young people of school age took to the streets to demonstrate their feelings about racism. Some commentators saw this as an act of independence, while others thought that the demonstrators were being manipulated by professional political organisations.

BETWEEN THE LINES

Read the newspaper feature article on pages 121–2 and then complete the following questions and activities.

7.1 In groups, research and write definitions for the following terms: political party, political platform, political agenda, left-wing politics, right-wing politics, communism, racism, the Resistance organisation and the One Nation party. Divide the terms between the groups in the class and then report your findings and definitions to the whole class.

(continued p. 123)

1. After years of criticism for apathy, Australia's school students have taken to the streets, exploding the notion that our youth don't give a hoot about politics. **STEPHANIE PEATLING** reports.

PolitiKids

2. The passion seems to have been lurking below the surface, waiting quietly for a trigger. Just two weeks ago, anti-racism rallies drew 10 000 schoolchildren out of the classrooms and onto the streets. Thousands of others joined the throng outside the opening of the Queensland State Parliament, rallied against the proposed mine at Jabiluka and chanted against the Government's waterfront reforms.

3. But instead of congratulations for leaving their TVs and computer games, their new activism has sparked attack for missing school, and insults for resorting to radical action.

4. The newly elected One Nation MP, Shaun Nelson, who at twenty-five could himself be called a youth activist, said: 'Putting children into the line of fire, into where there's going to be a sea of hatred and violence outside Parliament House, is child abuse. Using children to get across their political agenda is abhorrent. These communists should have to answer for their actions for doing this.'...

5. But the idea that youth are unable to think for themselves and are being manipulated by adults only increases their anger.

6. Sean Healy, twenty-six, is the national co-ordinator of Resistance, the group behind the anti-racism rallies, and says this opinion is not only ill-informed, but hypocritical. 'It is young people and school-age students who are the least likely to be brainwashed. They're less cynical than uni students and they haven't formed an attachment to a major political party. They don't have family responsibilities and they haven't spent years in a mind-destroying job.

7. 'If you're under eighteen, you aren't supposed to have any political opinions one way or the other. It's completely hypocritical because the people who were down on youth for being apathetic and not interested in politics are now the ones criticising their actions.'

8. It is a wave of action that has heartened Senator Natasha Stott Despoja, the closest thing Australia has to a youth-focused politician, who believes the political version of the old saying that children should be seen and not heard is definitely on the way out.

9. 'It's just so encouraging to see this sort of grassroots action. The racism rallies are certainly a focus point, but when you also look at the Jabiluka protests you can see there's a whole movement appearing.

10. 'In the last few weeks I've been flooded with e-mails and letters from school students who aren't even old enough to join a political party. And they're asking for the platforms of all the political parties, not just the Democrats, precisely because they do want to make up their own minds.'

11. But whether these protests are the beginnings of a broader

Patience and anger ... school students stage anti-racist protests against One Nation

youth protest is unclear. Professor Stuart Rees, the director of the Centre for Peace and Conflict Studies at the University of Sydney, believes youth is faced with so many concerns that it is difficult for it to unite around one particular issue. 'It's like a growing sense of disillusionment and a perception that they're being screwed. There's all sorts of things provoking young people like the reintroduction of upfront fees, the youth allowance, rising levels of suicide and all of it is the government saying we don't care about you. These protests we are seeing at the moment are just one piece of the jigsaw. The dilemma is whether conflict and protest can ever be a political movement.' ...

12 Professor Geoffrey Sherington, Dean of the Faculty of Education at the University of Sydney, believes the current protests are comparable with the anti-Vietnam movement thirty years ago, which he sees as the most successful historical example of youth action. 'They were very much organised around one issue and there were certainly a lot of school-age protesters as there are now. Then, as now, it seemed to attract kids whose parents had been involved with left-wing causes in their youth.'

13 Professor Sherington places the current protests in the context of international examples, such as the unemployment rallies in Germany at the beginning of the 1990s. He also points to the significant participation of Indonesian students in the end of the Soeharto regime earlier this year and the role of Chinese students in anti-government activism.

14 'But these incidents, especially in Germany, just died away and failed to become broader political movements addressing youth issues. What makes what's going on here so interesting is racism as the starting point and the activism of ethnic students who have obviously been directly affected by it ...

15 'We don't want to discourage students from taking an interest in politics and in an important issue like this. But as a parent, I was concerned about seeing schoolkids of twelve or thirteen being manhandled by the police,' says Duncan McInnes, the executive officer with the Parents Council.

16 'It's not a badge of courage to have a police record at that age. We aren't advising parents one way or the other, but we do think it's a good idea if they provide their students with a note if they are going to protests in school time, so that the school is covered.'

17 But according to Sean Healy, it was school students who pushed for the rallies to take place and Resistance is planning another day of action for 28 August, based on their initial success.

18 'At least a quarter of our membership is made up of high school students and they demanded the last protest because they were so furious about the rise of racism in Australia and because they felt no-one was listening to them,' Healy says ...

19 Or as Professor Rees puts it: 'It's like someone has been force-feeding all the youth valium for however many years and they're just now beginning to wake up to what is being done to them.'

Sydney Morning Herald,
10 August 1998

7.2 The headline of the article, PolitiKids, is a:
  a slang word
  b portmanteau word
  c pun
  d metaphor.

> **7.2** Definitions of 'slang', 'pun' and 'metaphor' appear in the Key Terms section of the Appendix.

> **7.2** Use your dictionary to look up unfamiliar words.

7.3 Paragraph 3 suggests that students should be congratulated for leaving their TVs and computer games because:
  a TV and computer games are violent
  b radical action is always good
  c TV and computer games do not teach students about politics
  d kids are usually criticised for being passive.

7.4 The phrase closest in meaning to 'resorting to radical action' (paragraph 3) is:
  a shouting and screaming on the streets
  b using confronting behaviour to make a point
  c taking the bull by the horns
  d using violence as a form of protest.

7.5 Sean Healy gives four reasons why students are least likely to be brainwashed (paragraph 6). Discuss the reasons and then explain them in your own words.

7.6 Write a multiple-choice question about the meaning of 'apathetic' (paragraph 7).

> **7.6** Refer to the Appendix for guidelines on multiple-choice questions.

7.7 'Growing sense of disillusionment' (paragraph 11) means:
  a gradual realisation that illusions are real
  b ideas of disenchantment
  c increasing awareness that something is false
  d enlarging sense of perception.

7.8 List the things that Professor Rees believes are provoking young people (paragraph 11).

7.9 The last sentence in paragraph 11 suggests that conflict and protest:
  a are equated with political movement
  b might be equated with political movement
  c will never be equated with political movement
  d should be equated with political movement.

7.10 'Professor Sherington places the current protests in the context of international examples' (paragraph 13) means that he is:
  a suggesting they are the same
  b suggesting they are different
  c separating them from each other
  d relating them to each other.

7.11 The opinions of various organisations and expert commentators are quoted in the article. List them and explain each opinion in one sentence.

INDEPENDENCE

7.12 Quote two pieces of evidence that suggest the student protests are based on racism.

7.13 What is the purpose of the article?

7.14 The best way to describe the article is:
   a balanced and thoughtful
   b informative but biased
   c informative and factual
   d factual and serious.

7.15 Write three or four lines explaining the reasons for your answer to 7.14.

7.16 Study the photograph on page 121. Write eight or ten lines describing its composition and explaining what it may suggest about the student protest.

> 7.16 Refer to the Appendix for guidelines on analysing visual texts before answering this question.

7.17 Writing

Study the photograph on page 122 and write a conversation between the Austral-asian student and the elderly lady with the umbrella.
   Either use the following opening lines:
Elderly lady: I would never have behaved like this when I was your age!
Student: But you didn't have anything to lose.
OR
In pairs, each write one side of the conversation. You could role play your conversation in class.

listening

8 on your OWN

presentation **School's out**

BETWEEN THE LINES

> 8.1 Refer to the Appendix for guidelines on listening tasks before you attempt this activity.

8.1 Use writing activities 5.6 and 5.7 (page 118) as the stimulus material for a listening activity. Choose one or two pieces of student work, tape them and have students prepare questions in groups.

CHOICES

chapter 6

We make choices every day. Over the years young people have been presented with an increasing amount of choice relating to careers, leisure, beliefs and relationships. This final chapter is concerned with some of the choices you will have once you leave school.

You will be reading:
- poems
- an official form
- an autobiography
- feature articles
- a newspaper report
- a personal letter
- non-fiction.

Writing activities include:
- a formal letter
- a biography
- a survey
- a report
- a poetry analysis.

1. **PRINCES AND PRINCESSES**
   Ruth Trowbridge
   'Between the Lines'
   Janet Hawley
   'The prince's bride'

2. **TRAVEL**
   Australian passport application
   Dugald Jellie
   'Have visa, will work'
   Overseas student

3. **ISSUES AND OPINIONS**
   Peter Kogoy
   'Teenagers say yes to sport drugs'

4. **BELIEFS**
   John Marsden
   Secret Men's Business

5. **EVALUATION**
   Peter Porter
   'A Consumer's Report'

6. Listening
   ACROSS THE DESERT
   Robyn Davidson
   Tracks

1 PRINCES and princesses

poem — **Ruth Trowbridge**
'Between the Lines'

Is the perfect partner still one of the most important choices we ever make?

> Don't tell me again that one day
> Prince Charming will arrive.
> I remember all those fairy tales—
> Only too well.
> 5 Who could take seriously
> Some guy who'd spend half his life
> Searching for thornless roses in the snow?
> Or travelling east of the sun and west of the moon?
> Or trying to climb glass mountains?
> 10 His reward is to marry the fair princess
> (Whose opinion is never asked)
> And live happily ever after.
> But what about the princess?
> What's her reward?
> 15 He gets to quaff mead with his cronies,
> Open Parliament,
> And show everyone the picture of him
> Standing on the dragon's head.
> She gets to keep a drafty castle clean,
> 20 Plan the banquets,
> Have the babies,
> And keep from screaming every time someone says,
> 'Is your husband *the* Prince Charming?
> You lucky girl!'
> 25 Personally, I'd rather wait for Rumpelstiltskin,
> At least, he'll expect me to think.

BETWEEN THE LINES

1.1 How do you know that the writer does not think much of the men whose activities are described in lines 7 to 9?

1.2 Line 11 is in parentheses (brackets). Why?

1.3 What differences does the poet see between the prince's life and the princess's?

1.4 Look up the story of 'Rumpelstiltskin'. Explain why she would rather wait for him than for Prince Charming.

1.5 Why is the poem entitled 'Between the Lines'?

1.6 The poet's attitude could be described as:
   a good humoured
   b irritated and bitter
   c irritated and amused
   d angry and sarcastic.

1.7 Explain your answer to 1.6 with evidence from the poem.

1.8 The language of the poem is:
   a poetic
   b formal
   c conversational
   d learned.

1.9 Explain your answer to 1.8 with evidence from the poem.

1.10 Explain exactly what is being satirised in the poem.

> **1.10** A definition of 'satire' appears in the Key Terms section of the Appendix.

Janet Hawley
'The prince's bride'

magazine feature article

This is the story of a young Australian girl who chose to marry a real Prince Charming in the late 1970s.

The prince's bride

1 It has all the makings of a fairy story: young Australian teacher has holiday romance with handsome Balinese prince. And then they marry. Two decades on, the protagonists talk to JANET HAWLEY about the realities of cultural difference.

2 Jane Gillespie was an adventurous twenty-four-year-old Australian schoolteacher when she married a Balinese prince and moved into his family palace at Ubud, the artistic centre of Bali, twenty years ago. Their elaborate wedding ceremony, with Hindu priests and gamelan orchestra, made the cover of the old *Women's Weekly*, with the bride called our 'exotic princess'.

3 The royal family changed her name to Asri Kerthyasa and gave her the title Jero (insider) as wife of Tjokorde (prince) Raka Kerthyasa, the second son of Tjokorde Ngurah and his tenth wife.

4 The twenty-four-year-old prince had grown up steeped in his cultural and ceremonial obligations, but had also travelled abroad and was outward-looking. He perceived Bali was about to undergo vast changes as the tourist throngs approached ...

5 [Asri says] 'We all thought Bali was paradise on earth, a Shangri-la jewel of an island better than Hollywood could dream up. Everything seemed so beautiful and tranquil, the harmonious landscape of terraced rice paddies, giant volcanoes, coconut palms and temples; the people all seemed so friendly and to love each other, walking peacefully around hand in hand, bathing naked in streams. It was, this sensual, fragrant, fertile, enchanting utopia ...

6 'But it didn't take long before reality hit!' [Asri] remembers the exact day when it struck her: 'Oh, so Balinese people don't all like each other! It's not perfect! People gossip, run each other down, get jealous, hate, manipulate and feel revengeful, just like us—just like people in all societies.' She was soon shedding tears of

frustration, striving to be the dutiful new wife, fitting in with other members of the large royal family and routine life in the palace compound.

7   'Balinese are obsessive and perfectionist about everything they do. I'd spend eternal hours learning to make the ritual daily temple offerings, weaving the palm fronds into circular baskets, pinning together the right sequence of leaves and flowers with sticks, making coloured rice shapes—then the tut-tutting old ladies' nimble fingers would unravel everything I did and do it all again …

8   'You're expected to toe the line all the time and it is so easy to sour your reputation by innocently doing the wrong thing, like speaking to another man or visiting someone alone. Raka told me at the start—remember, a million eyes are always watching you—and it's so true.

9   'After five years, I reached a point where I knew I was in danger of losing myself. I thought—they've changed my name, changed my religion to Hindu, they want me to dye my hair black so I look more Balinese, now they want to ceremonially file my teeth. No-one ever asks me what I want, what I think. It's just 100 per cent constant instruction: you fit in with us and our culture. I quite liked being the person I was before, when I was Jane Gillespie, and I didn't want to lose sight of that person.

10   'I fled on the plane back to Sydney and Raka came after me, and we started to do some major sorting out, which is ongoing.'

11   Nearly all that first wave of Australian–Balinese marriages failed. 'I think Raka and I are the only ones still married from that first era,' says Asri …

12   Raka points out that it is one thing to visit Bali as a tourist and sigh you'd love to stay there forever, but a very different commitment to become Balinese and adopt the local lifestyle. He's a gentle, sensitive, bright-witted man who admires his wife's strong spirit, while constantly espousing his philosophy of tolerance and harmony in all things.

13   'Balinese tradition is that men are regarded as very important, with freedom to do as much as they wish while wives take a deferential role,' he says.

14   'Many are like slaves,' Asri interrupts.

15   'Australian women are liberated, independent individuals, outspoken,' Raka continues. 'It's hard

Family life: Asri and Raka at home with two of their children, Max and Maya, who is learning to play the gamelan.

for Balinese men to accept this, and hard for Western women to accept that, when they marry a Balinese man, they also marry his extended family and his community, with numerous obligations and restrictions. Many Australian brides felt smothered by this …'

16   Life is easier now for Asri as she has her own defined role, running a small, high-quality hotel, The Ibah, which the couple built three years ago in a valley near the Ubud bridge on land Raka owned …

17   Some Balinese royal families are wealthy, with large landholdings, others have become impoverished, 'and many palaces are hardly palatial', Asri adds cheerfully. Inside the walled compound of the Ubud palace are numerous traditional, single-story pavilion houses with large verandahs, set in their own walled gardens, and many small stone temples. Some pavilions, such as the one in which their wedding ceremony took place, are highly ornate, with elaborate carvings and gold leaf decoration.

18   'Others, like the one where we lived for the first years of our marriage, are very simple,' remarks Asri. 'It's been modernised now, but twenty years ago our little home was typical of all homes in Ubud. We had no electricity, no refrigeration, no running water, no telephone, no radio or TV and a hard dirt floor that you could sweep like concrete. We used oil lamps, kerosene stoves; every morning you'd wake up to the roosters crowing and the whoosh of the water boy refilling your cold dipper bath with buckets he'd carry on a shoulder pole from the river. We used another dipper of water to flush the squat loo.

19   'For the first few months I'd lie awake half the night, listening to Raka's stepmother next door,

hitting rats with a rolled-up newspaper. Thank God we never had rats. There was a pig pen nearby and you'd hear them oinking, and pet peacocks paraded around the garden.

20 'I was young, healthy and freshly in love, so none of this worried me—I thought it was all wildly romantic and I was determined to learn everything I could to fit in.' The first huge culture clash hit when Asri went into the local hospital at Denpasar for the birth of her first baby. 'I was going to do the right thing, give birth in Bali, even though the health care was extremely basic. I had an extremely difficult time I swore I would never repeat, so I flew back to Australia for my next two births.

21 'When we took our first baby home, Raka's mother and the aunts were waiting on our veranda day and night, to take the precious first born son over. No-one had warned me that this was their traditional way. I was expected to hand the royal baby largely into their care and it was vital not to break this rule.

22 'In my headstrong way, the ferociously protective new young mother with my Australian standards of baby care and a degree in early childhood, I looked at my Balinese mother-in-law: a wonderful, highly traditional woman, but the red betel nut juice was dribbling down her lips as she chewed away, dirt was ingrained under her long fingernails and I couldn't surrender my newborn baby to her. I locked myself inside with the baby prince and poor Raka had to play diplomat again. It was extremely difficult for him as our son was regarded as the reincarnation of Raka's father and I'd put myself in the bad books more than I knew. I know now that I deeply hurt and offended my mother-in-law at the time, and it was at great cost to myself. Many in the royal family never forgave me and either began ignoring me or plotting against me ...'

23 Asri began spending more time back in Australia, teaching again while her first two sons completed part of their education in Sydney, then back to Bali in school holidays. Raka periodically joined her in Sydney, but underwent his own major culture adjustment ...

24 Six years ago, Asri made a commitment to live full-time in Bali. She gave birth to her third child, daughter Maya, and helped set up the bilingual school in Sanur. 'My second son is doing his HSC this year, in Bali, by correspondence, along with a group of Balinese–Australian students. Parents pay for a tutor, but it's a hard haul ...'

Wedding frocks and culture shocks: Jane Gillespie (now Asri), the 'naive young romantic', at her royal wedding in 1978.

25 Asri is happier now she has worked out her own balance of living in Bali, and is very busy, training local staff and managing their hotel. 'Bali is a fascinating island, but I no longer look at it through rose-coloured glasses, and I think that is a healthier perspective. I try to fit into the community and respect the culture, I wear traditional, formal Balinese clothes when necessary and do whatever I can to help Raka with ceremonies and his duties in Ubud. He is involved with so many groups and committees—environment, planning, culture, the museum, and I'm pleased to be able to help. But I'm also going to stay me.'

Good Weekend, 18 July 1998

BETWEEN THE LINES

Use your dictionary to look up unfamiliar words.

1.11 The marriage between Jane Gillespie and Tjokorde (prince) Raka Kerthyasa was possible because Raka:
  a was well-travelled and outward-looking
  b was captivated by Jane
  c had no respect for his culture
  d could see a tourist opportunity.

1.12 Marrying Balinese boys was popular because:
  a Bali was a beautiful place
  b the place and the relationships seemed utopian
  c the Australian girls didn't like Australian men
  d the Balinese were friendly and loved each other.

1.13 Explain the reasons why most Australian–Balinese marriages failed.

1.14 Decide whether the following statements are true or false.
  a The culture clashes arose because the Australian girls were naive.
  b Balinese people are always peaceful and harmonious.
  c The Balinese women were patient with Asri.
  d Raka warned Asri that she would be watched.

1.15 Asri's comment that she felt in danger of 'losing herself' (paragraph 9) means that she thought she would lose her:
  a looks
  b name
  c personality
  d identity.

1.16 List the reasons why Asri rejects the help of her mother-in-law.

1.17 Their son was regarded as 'the reincarnation of Raka's father' (paragraph 22) because:
  a the Balinese were old-fashioned
  b the Balinese were gullible
  c religion was important to the Balinese
  d the Balinese had silly beliefs.

1.18 Write ten or twelve lines about what Asri has done to fit in with the Balinese culture and way of life.

1.19 'I no longer look at it (Bali) through rose-coloured glasses' (paragraph 25) means:
  a Asri doesn't think of Bali in terms of romantic sunsets
  b Asri no longer regards Bali as perfect
  c Asri's view used to be unhealthy
  d Asri fits into the culture.

1.20 Study the photograph of Asri and Raka at home with their family (page 128). What features of the photograph illustrate the blend of cultures?

1.21 Writing

Interview a school friend or family friend who has come from a cultural background that is different from your own. Write up your interview as a report for your school newspaper. Remember to prepare questions to ask your friend before the interview.

2 TRAVEL

Australian passport application

form

Many young people choose to celebrate their independence by travelling and working overseas rather than concentrating on study and work at home. First, you need a passport.

BETWEEN THE LINES

Study the form on pages 133–6 and then complete the following questions and activities.

Page 1 of the form is shown on page 133, page 2 of the form is shown on page 134, page 3 of the form is shown on page 135 and page 4 of the form is shown on page 136.

2.1 After reading the top of page 1 of the form, decide whether the following statements are true or false.
   a You are likely to be able to obtain a Passport Application at a Post Office.
   b The person who fills in the Proof of Identity Declaration can be anyone who knows you.
   c You must prove you are an Australian citizen.
   d The 'documents which prove your name' refer to Birth Certificates and passports.
   e You need to provide un-expired passports.
   f You need two photographs.
   g There is no fee.
   h The card with the number on it on the top right-hand corner is for your convenience.

2.2 Why would you need to provide your mother's family name at her birth? (Refer to page 1 of the form.)

2.3 You leave the address label (bottom right-hand corner, page 1) blank if:
   a you want your passport sent to you
   b someone else is applying for you
   c you are going to collect your passport
   d you do not have a black ballpoint pen.

2.4 The phrase 'not required under legislation' (page 2) means:
   a the law on this point is unclear
   b there is no law that says you have to do it
   c it does not have to be legible
   d there is nothing in the fine print.

2.5 Discuss the wording of the Applicant's Declaration (page 2). Explain why you think the information would be useful for Commonwealth Agencies and the Australian Federal Police.

2.6 Decide whether the following statements are true or false. If you are under eighteen years of age, to obtain a passport you must:
   a have parental consent under all circumstances
   b produce a Death Certificate for a deceased parent
   c be able to produce your Birth Certificate
   d obtain consent, and if you cannot there is nothing you can do.

2.7 If you do not understand some of the occupations listed under 'People who can complete the Proof of Identity Declaration' (page 3), research them. Examples include Bailiffs, Clerks of Courts, Clerks of Petty Sessions and Stipendiary Magistrates.

2.8 Have a class discussion about the list of occupations on page 3. Which occupations are not mentioned? Can you think of reasons why they are not? Are there any circumstances under which a plumber, for example, could sign a Proof of Identity Declaration?

2.9 If you are unable to take your application to a Post Office in person (page 4), you:
   a cannot have an Australian passport
   b are not eligible for a limited validity passport
   c may be eligible for a limited validity passport
   d should not apply for an Australian passport.

2.10 If you were born in Australia on 20 August 1984 you must provide:
   a an original full Birth Certificate plus evidence that one parent was an Australian citizen or a Permanent Resident at that time
   b an original full Birth Certificate showing the names of both parents
   c evidence that both your parents are Australian citizens whether or not they were born in Australia
   d an original certificate showing that you are an Australian citizen.

2.11 Decide whether the following statements are true or false.
   a Photographs must be recent and clear.
   b Photographs can be any size.
   c The person who is vouching for you has to write his/her name only on the back of each photograph.
   d If you wear head covering for religious reasons, you may wear it in the photograph.
   e You cannot wear sunglasses.

2.12 You or your teacher can obtain a current Australian passport application form from a Post Office.

2.12 In groups, discuss this form. Do you think it is clear and well laid out? Make a list of the features you would change and then design an alternative form. Compare your form with the current Australian passport application form.

Department of Foreign Affairs and Trade
AUSTRALIAN PASSPORT APPLICATION*
Please do not use this form after July 1998

TO GET A PASSPORT, YOU NEED TO:
- Apply in person at a Post Office or Passport Office with a completed form. If you apply at a Post Office it may be necessary to make an appointment
- Have someone else fill in the Proof of Identity Declaration on page 3
- Show proof that you are an Australian citizen (see page 4)
- Show us documents which prove your name (see page 4)
- Provide any un-expired Passports
- Give us 2 photographs (see page 4)
- Pay the fee (fee is subject to change)

Passport Information Service
If you have any questions about how to get a passport
TELEPHONE 131 232 from anywhere in Australia.

AUSTRALIA POST
You may receive your new passport more quickly by applying at an Australian Post Office (you may need to make an appointment)

RETAIN THIS CARD

For enquiries quote this number: ***39873487 L***

See over for enquiries

39873487 L

IMPORTANT: If you are filling in this form for someone else, remember to show their details and not yours.

DETAILS ABOUT PERSON NEEDING A PASSPORT

Have you been issued with an Australian passport or other travel document since 1980? ☐ Yes ☐ No

If yes, write details of your most recent Australian Passport or travel document. | Letter | Number |

Tick type of passport required:
- ☐ Standard Passport — 32 visa pages
- ☐ Frequent Traveller Passport — 64 visa pages (extra cost)

PLEASE USE BLOCK LETTERS EXCEPT FOR SIGNATURES

Field	Family name	Given names
Name to appear in passport		
Name on full Birth Certificate		
Name on Certificate of Citizenship (if applicable)		

If the name to be shown on the new passport is different from the name shown on the document which proves you are an Australian citizen, you must show us other documents that explain the name change; for example a Marriage Certificate or a Deed Poll.

Date of Birth (appears in Passport): Day / Month / Year

Sex (appears in Passport): Male or Female

Place of Birth (appears in Passport): Town or City | Country of Birth

Home address: No. & Street | STD Home telephone | Suburb or Town or City | Postcode | STD Work telephone

Mother's family name at her birth: Family name only

OFFICIAL USE — List all OTHER names used

LABEL INSTRUCTIONS

- If you lodge your application at a Passport Office and want to collect your passport leave the Name/Address label blank, otherwise write your name and home address on the label and it will be sent by Receipted Delivery
- The applicant (not a person signing for the applicant) must sign both blank signature labels using a ballpoint pen (preferably black) taking care to stay within the labels; OR
- If the applicant is unable to sign, put a line through both signature labels

NAME / ADDRESS LABEL

NAME

ADDRESS

UNABLE TO SIGN

SIGNATURE LABELS

Certifying/Interviewing Officer	Issue authorised	Receipt number	Amount
(print name) (sign) / /	/ /		$

CHOICES 133

IN CASE OF EMERGENCY

If you want the Department to contact someone in the case of an emergency, this section should be completed. This information is not required under legislation and is purely voluntary.

Family name		Relationship		Home or business address	
STD	Home telephone	STD	Work telephone		Postcode

CITIZENSHIP OF ANOTHER COUNTRY

Are you a citizen of another country ☐ Yes ☐ No
If yes, give details

Country	Date acquired / /	How acquired

APPLICANT'S DECLARATION

I declare that the statements made in this application are true and correct. I understand that some or all of the information provided on this form will routinely be disclosed to Commonwealth Agencies responsible for immigration, customs and electoral registration, and to the Australian Federal Police. I give consent for enquiries to be made with the Department of Immigration and Multicultural Affairs regarding my citizenship if necessary.

Signature of the applicant or the person signing for the applicant   Date

False or misleading statements may be subject to penalties in accordance with the Passports Act 1938

IF YOU ARE UNDER 18 YEARS THE FOLLOWING SECTION MUST ALSO BE COMPLETED

Marriage details (tick where applicable)

Now married ☐   Previously married ☐   Never married ☐

Consent to issue by parents

If you have never been married we need the consent of every person who has parental responsibility for you. In most cases these would be the people shown on your Birth Certificate as parents.

If you are now married or have been married, you do not need consent, but you must show us your Marriage Certificate.

- You must show us your Birth Certificate with the names of your parents on it, even if you hold a previous passport or were born overseas.
- If your parent has died, you must show us the Death Certificate.
- If a Court Order altering parental responsibility has been made, you must show us the Order.
- If consent is given by a parent whose name is now different from the name on your Birth Certificate, you must show us documents that explain their name change.
- If you cannot obtain a consent, please contact us for advice.

I give my consent for the issue of a passport to

Name to appear in passport

CONSENT BY FATHER

Family name		Given names	
No.	Street		
Suburb or Town or City			Postcode
STD	Home telephone	STD	Work telephone

Signature of father in **presence of witness**

	Date / /

CONSENT BY MOTHER

Family name		Given names	
No.	Street		
Suburb or Town or City			Postcode
STD	Home telephone	STD	Work telephone

Signature of mother in **presence of witness**

	Date / /

Consent must be witnessed by someone other than the child's mother, father, sister, brother.

WITNESS TO FATHER'S SIGNATURE

Family name		Given names	
Signature			Date / /
STD	Home telephone	STD	Work telephone

WITNESS TO MOTHER'S SIGNATURE

Family name		Given names	
Signature			Date / /
STD	Home telephone	STD	Work telephone

PAGE 2

PROOF OF IDENTITY

To help us identify the person needing the passport, we need someone else to complete the Proof of Identity Declaration below. This person:
- must NOT be related by birth or marriage
- must have known you for at least one year
- must be currently employed in one of the professional or occupational groups below
- must be easily contactable by telephone during normal working hours
- must write on the back of both photographs "This is a true photograph of ...(*applicant's name in full*)..." and sign their name
- must be an Australian citizen (unless you are applying overseas)

PEOPLE WHO CAN COMPLETE THE PROOF OF IDENTITY DECLARATION (Occupation Groups)

1. Accountants - members of the (1A) Institute of Chartered Accountants in Australia, (1B) Australian Society of Certified Practicing Accountants, (1C) National Institute of Accountants, (1D) Association of Taxation and Management Accountants, (1E) Registered Tax Agents (specify which below)
2. Bailiffs
3. Bank Managers except Managers of bank travel centres
4. Barristers, Solicitors and Patent Attorneys
5. Chartered Professional Engineers
6. Clerks of Courts
7. Clerks of Petty Sessions
8. Members currently serving in the regular Australian Defence Force with at least five years continuous service
9. Dentists
10. Registered Medical Practitioners
11. Elected representatives of Federal, State and Territory Parliaments, Legislative Assembly of Norfolk Island and Municipal or Shire Councils
12. Holders of Statutory Offices for which an annual salary is payable
13. Judges
14. Members of the Chartered Institute of Company Secretaries in Australia
15. Marriage Celebrants
16. Pharmacists
17. Police Officers with at least five years continuous service
18. Postal Managers
19. Public Servants - current full-time employees of Commonwealth, State, Territory or Local Governments or Statutory Authorities, who have been employed continuously for at least five years by their current employer
20. Sheriffs
21. Stipendiary Magistrates
22. Teachers - full time who have been teaching for more than five years at schools or tertiary institutions
23. Registered Veterinary Surgeons
24. Registered Nurses

PROOF OF IDENTITY DECLARATION

I declare that I have known
FULL NAME OF APPLICANT

Family name	Given names

for [ ] *year(s) and vouch for his/her identity. I have endorsed the back of both photographs. I have given my details in the section opposite.*

Signature _____ Date ___/___/___

DETAILS OF PERSON SUPPLYING THIS DECLARATION.

Family name	Given names
Sex (not mandatory)	Date of Birth (not mandatory)
Home or business address	Postcode
STD Home telephone	STD Work telephone
Australian passport number (if you have one)	Occupation group number (as above)

OFFICIAL USE ONLY

Document	Doc. No.	Date of Issue	Place of Issue	Details	Att	Ret
Birth certificate (show full names)				App		
				Father		
				Mother		
Previous passport						
Citizenship document						
Parent res. cit. status						
Details of name change (include document type - eg. marriage certificate, statutory declaration)						
Court order/ Death certificate						
Identity documents (check signature)						
Notes						

Lodged by: ☐ Self ☐ Father ☐ Mother ☐ Other ....
App: ☐ PICS ☐ CC ☐ E/R ☐ Tel ☐ Known
POID: ☐ ☐ ☐ ☐ ☐

WHAT TO DO NEXT

Take this form to any Post Office or Passport Office in Australia, or Australian Diplomatic Mission overseas.

- If you take it to a Post Office, **it may be necessary to make an appointment.**
- If you are under 18 years and not married, a parent or certain other persons can take the form in for you. Phone 131 232 for further information.
- If you are unable to lodge your application in person because of distance, you may be eligible for the issue of a limited validity passport. In Australia, you should phone 131 232 for advice. If you are overseas you should contact the nearest Australian Diplomatic Mission.
- For information on the present passport fees and acceptable methods of payment, please phone 131 232 for advice in Australia, or phone any Australian Diplomatic Mission overseas.

When you go to lodge your application, please check that you have:

- a completed form
- the document† that proves you are an Australian citizen
- the document† that proves your present name and additional documents for any name changes, eg. Marriage Certificate(s), Deed Poll etc
- your current valid passport, if you have one
- your 2 photographs, both endorsed and signed by the person who filled in the Proof of Identity Declaration on page 3
- fee for your passport; cash or cheque (payable to 'The Collector of Public Moneys')
- other documents† that show your name to confirm who you are, eg. driver's licence, credit cards, rate notices, household accounts etc. We may require you to provide further documents if those you have provided are not acceptable.

PROOF OF CITIZENSHIP

You must show us a document† which proves that you are an Australian Citizen. This can be:

- An Australian passport† of more than 2 years validity issued after 22 November 1984, OR
- If born in Australia

    before 20 August 1986, a full Birth Certificate† showing the names of both parents; OR

    on or after 20 August 1986, a full Birth Certificate† plus evidence that one parent was an Australian citizen or had Permanent Resident status at time of your birth. OR

- If you were born overseas:

    A certificate† showing Australian citizenship issued by the Department of Immigration and Multicultural Affairs. The certificate should show your name and date and place of birth. If your citizenship document does not show your place of birth, you will have to show us an official document† which does. Holders of Declaratory Certificates of Australian Citizenship issued prior to 1 December 1982 or between 16 April 1984 and 10 October 1984 should phone 131 232 for advice; OR

    If you do not hold proof of Australian citizenship, please contact the Department of Immigration and Multicultural Affairs.

†THE DOCUMENTS YOU PROVIDE MUST BE ORIGINALS AS SUPPLIED BY THE ISSUING AUTHORITY

PHOTOGRAPHS

We need 2 identical photographs of you. They must be:

- not more than 6 months old.
- a full front view of your head and shoulders without any head covering or tinted glasses. If you wear a head covering for religious reasons, we will accept a photograph which shows your facial features. If you normally wear prescription glasses, you should be wearing glasses with untinted lenses in the photograph. The photograph must have a plain, light coloured background.
- both photographs must be endorsed as set out in the Proof of Identity section on page 3.

We will not accept poor quality photographs. The photographs in your passport may appear slightly different from those supplied.

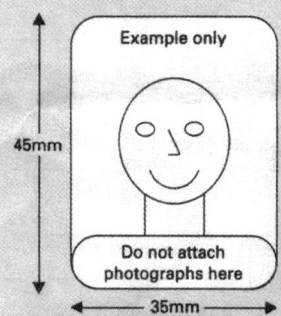

REMEMBER: If you have any questions about getting a passport, telephone our information service on 131 232 (from anywhere in Australia)

*The information which you provide is used to assess your eligibility for the issue of an Australian Passport and to maintain a data base of this information for use by the Department should you apply in the future for another Passport. The information you provide is a requirement of Regulation 5 of the Passports Regulations in force under the Passports Act 1938.

PCI (8/96)

Dugald Jellie
'Have visa, will work'

newspaper feature article

Having obtained your passport, you have several options.

Have visa, will work

1 Go West, young person. Or North, or East. There's a wealth of opportunity out there, just waiting to be seized.

2 EACH DAY, most of us travel to work. Many of us work to travel. But more of us should travel and work or work and travel. Which doesn't mean throwing in your office job to become a city bicycle courier, or flying at the front end of the plane, business class.

3 We're talking about working overseas, either long-term or short-term, doing volunteer service or teaching. The benefits are obvious: leisure travel may well broaden the mind, but it also depletes the bank balance. Especially now, while the Australian dollar is barely enough to buy you a small bag of mixed lollies in the United States.

4 With our currency bottomed-out to Banana Republic depths, it's almost an economic imperative to earn hard currency (especially US dollars) while you travel. It's time to combine the business of earning a quid (or a yen or a guilder or food and lodgings) with the pleasure of travel.

5 There are plenty of jobs going out there, especially for Australians, who have a hard-earned reputation for working hard on foreign soil and excelling at whatever they do.

6 Last weekend, for example, the first of more than 1200 Australians conscripted by Camp Counsellors USA to work on American summer camps headed abroad for a three-month stint during which they receive free accommodation and meals, and pocket money ranging from $1425 to $1500. A program co-ordinator with Camp Counsellors, Sophie Paterson, says eighteen to thirty year-old Australians are prized at the summer camps, with unlimited positions available.

7 'We sent over as many as applied,' says Paterson.

8 'They just can't get enough of Australian workers, probably because of their friendly attitude and because they have great outdoor skills to offer these kids. Australian childhoods are all about spending summers at the beach swimming and playing plenty of outdoor sport.'

9 Working at an American summer camp is just one option. There is a wealth of opportunity abroad. You could pull pints in a Glasgow pub, work as a chef in London, au pair in the US, harvest melons on a kibbutz in Israel, sub-edit on an English-speaking newspaper in Hong Kong, vaccinate kids in Kenya as a volunteer doctor for Medicins Sans Frontieres, plant trees in Canada, be a deckie on a cruise ship through the Caribbean, teach English to Korean businessmen, or pick mushrooms on a Swiss farm as a WWOOF (a Willing Worker on Organic Farms). The possibilities are endless.

10 And the number of Australians taking up those possibilities is increasing. Last year, 76 000 Australian citizens left to work overseas (or, at least, that's how many did so and told the Department of Immigration about it), compared with 41 500 in 1990.

11 FOR MOST Australians heading abroad to work and play, the easiest way to get a job is through the working holiday visa (WHV) program—a government-to-government scheme that allows citizens to work for limited periods in countries with reciprocal deals. (That's a diplomatic agreement that seeks to foster social and cultural ties between countries, with plenty of fine print involved) ...

12 The most popular WHV among Australians [is] for Britain ... Changes were made in October 1994 to tighten the scheme and establish more specific guidelines about what type of work is allowed. Not that it has stopped the tide of young Australians making the trip to London in search of work. It is a time-honoured tradition, popular already in the 1950s and the Swinging '60s, when Australians journeyed

to the mother country via the Suez Canal.

13 Applicants for the British WHV need to meet the following key criteria:
   • ...have Australian citizenship
   • be aged between seventeen and twenty-seven years
   • be visiting primarily for a holiday, not employment (you are not allowed to work for more than half your stay)
   • be single, or one of a married couple where both partners are otherwise eligible
   • if a parent, must undertake to leave Britain before the child turns five years of age
   • must be able to support and accommodate themselves without British welfare
   • must have funds totalling at least $3000
   • have to leave Britain at the end of the two-year residency permitted by the visa ...

14 But who says work opportunities stop as soon as you cross the borders of the seven WHV program countries? I've met a Sydney guy who worked in Bollywood, the film industry in Bombay (now known as Mumbai ...), making movies. Apparently, the Indians just lapped up his blue-eyed, blond-haired, matinée idol looks.

15 Similarly, modelling agencies in Hong Kong are always on the lookout for Western belles and beaus with the right stuff. And they pay handsomely, with wages up to $HK600 ($123) an hour ...

16 But not all Australians head abroad in search of hard currency.

17 Each year, thousands travel abroad to lend a helping hand in voluntary work, with activities ranging from picking citrus fruit in Cuba through the Australia–Cuba Friendship Society, to setting up basic infrastructure such as shelter, water supply and sanitation in Bangladesh through RedR Australia (Registered Engineers for Disaster Relief).

18 One group that offers a variety of volunteer activities is Australian Volunteers Abroad [AVA], with programs in about forty countries. This group works a bit differently from others, in that there is no volunteer fee and your plane tickets are paid. Volunteers receive a monthly stipend as well as a pre-departure allowance.

19 A recent study by AVA of 600 returned volunteers showed that, for most, the positives of their experience outweighed the negatives.

20 The benefits included gaining an understanding of another culture or society; personal development; the friendships made while on assignment; learning tolerance and a wider view of the world; changing career direction or professional development; the opportunity to assist less fortunate people; and gaining insights into Australian society and culture.

21 The study obviously failed to mention one more, fundamental, advantage of working overseas. It sure beats catching the 8.05 a.m. city-bound train each weekday, as you travel to work.

Sydney Morning Herald,
30 May 1998

Work program contacts

Camp America/Au Pair America
288a Whitehorse Road
Balwyn VIC 3103
Phone (03) 9899 5424

Camp Counsellors USA (CCUSA)
Level 7, 428 George St
Sydney NSW 2000
Phone (02) 9223 3366

Council on International Educational Exchange (CIEE)
Level 8, The University Centre
210 Clarence St
Sydney NSW 2000
Phone (02) 9373 2730

International Exchange Programs (IEP)
Level 5, 300 George St
Sydney NSW 2000
Phone (02) 9233 7111

Japan Exchange and Teaching Program (JET)
Embassy of Japan
112 Empire Circuit
Yarralumla ACT 2600
Phone (02) 6273 3244

International WWOOF
Lionel Pollard
c/o W Tree
via Buchan VIC 3885
Phone (03) 5155 0218

Medicins Sans Frontieres
GPO Box 5141
Sydney NSW 2001
Phone (02) 9319 3500

Kibbutz Program Desk
146 Darlinghurst Rd
Darlinghurst NSW 2010
Phone (02) 9360 6300

Australian Volunteers Abroad
PO Box 350
Fitzroy VIC 3065
Phone (03) 9279 1788

WORKING HOLIDAY VISAS

Country	Age	Max. time	Minimum funds required	Visa cost
Canada	18–25	12 months	$4000*	Nil
Ireland	18–25	12 months	Sufficient funds for at least initial period	Nil
Japan	18–30	18 months	$2500 for individuals/ $3500 for couples	Nil
Korea	18–25	12 months	$4000	$70
Malta	18–25	12 months	$4500	$51
Netherlands	18–25	12 months	$2000	Nil
UK	17–27	24 months	$3000	$78.30

Source: *Working Overseas: A Working Holiday Guide*, Global Exchange, rrp $19.95
* Need not all be cash, i.e. could include return ticket.

BETWEEN THE LINES

2.13 Find out what a visa is and write a definition of it.

2.14 Do you think the title is effective? Why or why not?

2.15 'Leisure travel ... depletes the bank balance. Especially now' (paragraph 3)? In your own words explain why.

2.16 Find out what a Banana Republic (paragraph 4) is and write a definition.

2.17 In groups, write multiple-choice questions for the phrases 'economic imperative', 'hard currency' (paragraph 4) and 'hard-earned reputation' (paragraph 5).

> **2.17** Refer to the Appendix for guidelines on writing multiple-choice questions.

2.18 'At least, that's how many did so and told the Department of Immigration about it' (paragraph 10) implies that:
  a possibly more than 76 000 Australians worked overseas
  b some of the Australians were not telling the truth
  c less than 76 000 Australians worked overseas
  d 76 000 Australians left, but they did not all work.

2.19 In paragraph 11, 'countries with reciprocal deals' in this context refers to:
  a countries who have complicated worker contracts
  b countries who trade workers
  c slightly dodgy arrangements between countries
  d countries with similar arrangements for visiting workers.

2.20 Other than the information in the table, what other details of the working holiday visa (WHV) for the UK are you given?

2.21 After studying the table on the WHV, decide whether the following statements are true or false.
  a The WHV for Japan could be the cheapest per person.
  b The WHV for Malta is the most expensive.
  c The WHV for the UK is the best value.
  d The minimum amount of money required for any country can include the cost of a return ticket.
  e A WHV for Ireland is the cheapest.

2.22 Paragraph 20 lists the benefits of the program. The last one is 'gaining insights into Australian society and culture'. Write ten or twelve lines explaining how you think travelling and working overseas may help you to gain an understanding of your own culture and society.

2.23 Writing

Write a letter requesting information from one of the contacts listed in the article. You will need to supply basic information about yourself as well as indicating your interests and skills. Explain exactly what type of work you are seeking and whether you want paid or voluntary work.

> **2.23** Refer to the Appendix for guidelines on letters.

letter

Overseas student

Here is an account from one student who travelled overseas to work and learn German.

> Room 34
> Goethe-Institut
> Merkelstrasse 4
> 37085 Göttingen
> Germany
>
> Dear Lucy
>
> 1 Having just spent eight weeks doing a typing course in New Zealand, I now arrive in Germany to find that half the letters on the keyboard are in a different place. Plus it's an old system, plus they don't use the same punctuation marks, so if anything looks odd, it's because I've had to compromise with the keyboard.
>
> 2 Seven days ago I arrived in the fairytale town of Göttingen, where the Brothers Grimm were actually professors. My room is on the top floor of a grand old heritage building with the most glorious view of quaint little cottages and sweeping green hills.
>
> 3 The gym scene didn't impress me too much so I'm holding aerobic classes at the Institute for staff and students. Next week the local gym is allowing me to teach a Step class Oz style. I absolutely LOVE studying the language and don't mind a bit the four hours of homework every night. (Wish I could have said the same for the HSC.) I have no idea where it all might lead, but at the moment I'm so happy, I don't think it matters.
>
> 4 Berlin, on the other hand, was a rather—what's the best word here?—trying/taxing/didactic/karmic experience. The city itself is captivating—bustling and beautiful and oozing with art, history, culture, music and construction sites! The Berliners are charging into the twenty-first century with Europe's largest building project well under way on Potsdamer Plaza. The city has more trees than Paris, more bridges than Venice and more than thirty pages of the telephone directory dedicated to Fitness Centres. Their Philharmonic Orchestra is probably the best in the world, and the food hall on the sixth floor of KaDeWe is mind boggling. Even the fact that street numbers run sequentially up one side of the street and down the other (and I was always at the wrong end) didn't bother me too much.
>
> 5 One of the best things about Germany is that they get all the latest movies from all over the world and then dub them. This dubbing is so well done that for the first half hour of *As Good As It Gets* I kept wondering where Jack Nicholson had learnt to speak German so well. It's fantastic for language learning.
>
> 6 I'm slowly getting used to some strange habits. For instance, take the simple scenario of crossing the street. Firstly, if there's no traffic light or pedestrian crossing, they won't even entertain the idea. If the light is red, then it doesn't matter whether it's two o'clock in the morning and there isn't a car in sight, they will NOT cross the road. And they'll give you a lecture if YOU cross the road. I've also been surprised by their apparent lack of

modesty. I was walking through some magnificent gardens in Potsdam (a town full of castles just outside Berlin) when I stumbled upon a nudist colony. They were all either lying or strolling or playing frisbee, completely in the nude. I presumed this was some strange anomaly until I went for a run in another park, this time in Berlin, and found exactly the same thing. But what impressed me the most was a sign in the bathroom of a mixed household in Marburg. It read: 'The females request that the male tenants sit down when urinating so as not to spray the toilet seat.' This was no private joke; this was meant in all earnestness.

7   Yugoslavia, on the other hand, is a different planet. I never thought I'd experience a bigger culture shock than India but Belgrade managed to astound, frustrate, depress and amaze me all in one breath. I wanted to send you a postcard but none were to be found—a reflection of the number of tourists to be seen. The buses were almost as crowded as Kenya (the only thing missing is the live chickens) and the driving is utterly chaotic. A German would not feel at home as traffic lights are the last things people think of when crossing the road. The city itself is overwhelmingly grey. All the buildings are in a chronic state of dilapidation and disrepair. The paintwork is peeling off grand old building after grand old building, reminiscent of tears streaming down a face. When I had my first roll of film developed I thought I'd inadvertently used black and white film. The place looks worn and withered and its state is reflected in the faces of the black-scarved women selling overripe bananas at the markets.

8   I've decided to stay in Göttingen. I can visit other cities on weekends. Plus, I'd love to have a go at teaching German. A woman approached me at gym this afternoon and asked me if I would teach an American student who has just arrived. Plus the gym has just offered me a couple of regular weekly, generously paid classes. Plus I'm having a ball. So I think destiny has it in for me here.

9   Time to do my homework!
All the best and love
Helena

BETWEEN THE LINES

2.24 Find out who the Brothers Grimm were (paragraph 2) and explain why Helena's description of Göttingen is appropriate.

2.25 Helena makes surprising contrasts in her description. Write down at least two examples from paragraphs 4 and 6.

2.26 Writing
Write about a page on the qualities of this letter. Before you begin, make notes on the conversational tone, the information, the descriptive qualities and the enthusiasm and sense of humour of the writer.

3 ISSUES and opinions

newspaper report

Peter Kogoy
'Teenagers say yes to sport drugs'

Young people are increasingly asked their opinion on a range of issues in our society. What do you think about the following issue?

WHAT THEY SAY

Q RACE FOR GOLD
Would you take a drug that would win you an Olympic gold medal at Sydney in 2000, make you a millionaire but kill you at forty?

Definitely **3%**
Probably **3%**
Unsure **5%**
Probably not **15%**
Definitely not **72%**

Q Given the choice, would you go to see Cathy Freeman run the 400 metre final or have a free day off school?

Freeman **40%**
Day off **50%**

MOST ADMIRED SPORTS STARS

BOYS

1 **Michael Jordan** (basketball)
2 **Anna Kournikova** (tennis)
3 **Greg Norman** (golf)
4 **Tiger Woods** (golf)
5 **Ronaldo** (soccer)
6 **Robert Harvey** (Rules)
7 **Pete Sampras** (tennis)
8 **Mark Waugh** (cricket)
9 **Martina Hingis** (tennis)
10 **Andrew John** (league)

 **GIRLS**

1 **Cathy Freeman** (athletics)
2 **Michael Jordan** (basketball)
3 **Pat Rafter** (tennis)
4 **Kieren Perkins** (swimming)
5 **Susie O'Neill** (swimming)
6 **Michael Klim** (swimming)
7 **Pete Sampras** (tennis)
8 **Martina Hingis** (tennis)
9 **Harry Kewell** (soccer)
10 **Samantha Riley** (swimming)

Teenagers say yes to sport drugs

1 Almost 60 per cent of teenagers would not rule out using performance enhancing drugs in sport if these were undetectable and safe, a survey has found.

2 Forty per cent would not rule out using performance enhancing drugs if they were safe or not, the *Inside Sport* magazine survey found.

3 The survey also asked more than 500 Year 11 students if they would take a drug that would win them an Olympic gold medal in Sydney and make them a millionaire but would kill them at forty.

4 Only 3 per cent said they would definitely go for gold and a further 3 per cent said they would probably take the drug because it would give them better performance and bigger muscles.

5 A seventeen-year-old boy said he would definitely use drugs 'to become a better person'.

6 From steroids 'people gain superhuman strength and speed, making them better people,' he said.

7 A sixteen-year-old boy, whose favourite sport was rugby league, said: 'Once you get selected in the side you want to be in and are making lots of money, you stop using them.'

8 A sixteen-year-old girl, whose favourite sports were hockey, swimming and skating, said she would probably use drugs 'just to have the experience of achieving something that I may not get otherwise.'

9   Others said they would use drugs only to overcome persistent injuries or in extreme circumstances, such as to be fit for a State of Origin match.

10 The students distinguished between performance enhancing drugs and recreational drugs, such as marijuana, which is included on the International Olympic Committee's list of banned substances.

11 To the question, 'Should athletes be penalised by sporting bodies for using marijuana, a drug which does nothing to enhance performance?' 66 per cent said 'probably not' or 'definitely not', 21 per cent said 'definitely' or 'probably' and 12 per cent were unsure.

12 To the final question on drugs, 'Do you personally know anyone who uses drugs to enhance their own performance?' 15 per cent said yes.

13 The results of the survey support a recent claim by Australian Olympic Committee chairman John Coates that about 4 per cent of NSW schoolchildren between the ages of eleven and seventeen were on steroids, double the rate of the general population.

14 A quarter of students surveyed said basketball was one of their favourite sports, with cricket and netball each popular with 21 per cent followed by soccer with 19 per cent.

15 Australian Rules and tennis were the next most popular with 15 per cent.

16 While girls were a little more realistic about their chances of making it big in the sporting arena, 25 per cent of boys responded by claiming they were good enough to make it at elite level.

17 Forty per cent of boys surveyed revealed they trained between five and nine hours a week in chasing sporting glory, while almost one in five set aside ten to fourteen hours a week for sporting activities.

18 Most of the teenagers thought sport stars, with the exception of footballers, were overpaid.

19 The only footballers to make it on the role models' list were dual St Kilda Brownlow medallist Robert Harvey and Newcastle's Andrew Johns.

20 Asked 'Is it a good thing that Sydney is hosting the next Olympics?', 87 per cent said 'definitely' or 'probably' and only 6 per cent were against it.

Sun-Herald, 4 October 1998

BETWEEN THE LINES

3.1 Study the graphic that accompanies the report. Represent the responses to the first question by constructing a pie graph.

3.2 What do you think the responses to the second question suggest about young people? Do you think it is a fair question? Discuss the issue in class before writing your answer.

> **3.2** Refer to the Appendix for guidelines on pie (or circle) graphs.

3.3 Paragraphs 3 to 8 of the report deal with the responses to the second question in the graphic. Three students and their responses are mentioned in paragraphs 5 to 8. Why do you think their particular comments are focused on rather than the responses of the 72 per cent who said 'definitely not'?

3.4 Do you think the message of the headline accurately reflects the information in the report? Give reasons for your answer.

3.5 Discuss the possible reasons why only five women are mentioned in the list of 'most admired sports stars'. List the reasons offered in class discussion and then write a letter to the organising body of your favourite sport suggesting ways in which they could encourage interest in sportswomen.

3.6 Writing

In groups, research one of the sports stars mentioned in the report or another sports star who is popular in your group. Prepare a brief biography, with illustrations if possible. Your biography should include an analysis of the reasons for your chosen sports star's popularity.

3.7 Writing

In groups, using the information in the report, prepare your own sport and drugs survey for a survey of your class, year or school to gauge attitudes to drugs in sport. Use the results to write a report for your school or class newspaper or newsletter.

4 BELIEFS

self-help book excerpt

John Marsden
Secret Men's Business

As the opening comment of this chapter suggested, choices do not just apply to which life partner you choose or which country you visit. Read the advice that John Marsden offers young men; although it could equally apply to young women and anyone else.

> Most young men in Australia today—and most adults—are in a very dangerous state. They have no spiritual belief.
> That doesn't mean I'm trying to convert you to any particular religion. I'm not. Nevertheless people who have a strong religious
> 5 belief may be better off than people who don't, in the short term anyway.
> In the long term it can be unhealthy to commit to a religious system that you haven't thought through yourself. In other words it's better to come to a set of beliefs because you honestly, truly
> 10 and deeply believe them, not because you've had them drummed into you all your life.
> Among the major belief systems that have been practised in Australia are the aboriginal belief system, the Christian one, and more recently the Jewish and Islamic ones.
> 15 As well, smaller numbers of people are committed to Buddhism, Hinduism, Shinto, Baha'i and other religions.
> The more you know about different religions, the better. The more you think about these issues, the better. At the end of your life you may not have come to any conclusion about God and religion,
> 20 but at least you've given it your best shot. The dangerous state I spoke of, having no spiritual belief, applies only to people who don't think about this stuff, who don't even look for religious truth.

There is no more important topic for human beings to
contemplate. Is there a God? Were we created or did we just
happen? Is there a purpose to our existence? Is there a life after
death? For as long as humans have existed we can be sure that
they have wondered about these matters. There has never been,
as far as we can tell, a society which has not believed in a god
or gods.

Maybe the problems we have in western society are partly a
result of our lack of belief. The fast growth of science has made us
question everything, and trust only logical explanations. Science
is dedicated to solving mysteries; religions are dedicated to maintaining them.

As well, many organised religions have done themselves
damage by insisting on silly and meaningless doctrine, or have
been damaged by their leaders' immoral activities.

Truth is truth, and if a religious leader steals money from his
followers or sexually assaults some of them, it doesn't mean that
the teachings of that religion are false. But it's not surprising that
people feel angry, disillusioned and betrayed in those circumstances.

Karl Marx argued that 'religion is the opiate of the masses';
in other words, religion was cynically used by powerful people to
keep the rest of the population under control. It was a drug that
tranquillised them, so they didn't realise how awful their lives
really were.

I don't know if that's true or not. I don't want to believe it,
but even if there is some truth in it, I think the picture is more
complicated than Marx suggested.

I suspect, though, that as religion has faded in importance for
many people, they have found other things to replace it. One of
the most obvious is sport. By becoming obsessed with sport, by
following a team or a player with avid interest, by watching sport
'religiously' on TV, people escape from the reality of their lives.

'I reckon he deserves it', they say, generously, of a player being
paid over $1 million dollars for losing the final of a tennis
tournament. 'If you ask me they earn every cent', they say of a
football team who gets $8 million dollars a season between them.

The speaker might be a panel beater with three children, who
has worked for fifteen years at his trade, who has the respect and
admiration of his workmates and neighbours, and the love of his
wife and children, who has nearly paid off half their suburban
house ...Yet he watches excitedly as a professional golfer lines up
a putt in a skins tournament that could add another $100 000 to
the golfer's $28 million fortune. And the panel-beater really cares!
It really matters to him that the golfer sinks the putt!

Why? Is he on a 10 per cent commission?

I don't think so.

This man seems to underestimate his own value.

In 1996 I published a book called *This I Believe*. Before I plug
it here I'd better point out that the profits from the book go to

the Save the Children Fund, so I'm not promoting it now to make money for myself. But I recommend *This I Believe* to you. It contains over 100 short essays, most of them by famous Australians, in which each person states the beliefs he or she holds. They range from radical to conservative, from religious to atheistic, from narrow to wide.

By browsing through a book like this you may get a clearer focus on your own beliefs.

After you've done that, try writing such a statement yourself.

Incidentally, the fact that you believe in something doesn't mean you're locked in for life. There's no virtue in having a closed mind. You should always be open to new ideas, prepared to rethink your position. That's proof that you're alive. 'I think, therefore I am,' said a famous French philosopher.

In a men's toilet in a restaurant in Fitzroy, Melbourne, I saw this piece of graffiti: 'Opinions should be held as lightly as a leaf on a window sill: blown in any direction by the slightest puff of wind.'

Not your average graffiti. But I liked it, although it's worth noting that opinions and beliefs are two different things.

I suspect that one of the greatest enemies for human beings is cynicism. To be cynical is to believe in nothing, to think the worst of everyone, to be certain that everybody's trying to rip you off. There's no good in the world, everyone's just out for their own interests.

There is overwhelming evidence that the world's not like that, but cynical people don't want to know about it. Cynicism is like gastro: it goes through your whole system and makes you shitty.

You often get gastro because you haven't been clean yourself: you haven't washed your hands after going to the toilet. You get cynical because you haven't been trustworthy and honest and decent yourself. You think that because you're pretty grubby, the rest of the world must be equally grubby. It isn't.

The opposite to cynicism is trust.

BETWEEN THE LINES

4.1 Decide whether the following statements are true or false. John Marsden expressed the following ideas.
 a The major belief systems practised in Australia are aboriginal, Christian, Jewish and Islamic.
 b Searching for religious truth is the important thing.
 c People are in danger if they don't think about beliefs.
 d There are more important topics than God.
 e All societies appear to have a belief in a god or gods.
 f Science is safer because it depends on logical explanations.
 g Religious leaders are above sin.
 h One rotten apple doesn't spoil the whole barrel.

4.2 Before you complete the following questions and activities, decide what is meant by words in the excerpt such as 'spiritual', 'religion', 'doctrine' and 'atheistic' and phrases such as 'organised religion' and 'belief system'.

4.3 John Marsden considers spiritual belief is:
  a only valuable in the short term
  b valuable if you have been brought up with it
  c valuable if you have thought it through
  d not valuable at all in the long term.

4.4 What explanation does Marsden give for the panel-beater's enthusiasm about golf?

4.5 Explain the comparison between opinions and a leaf (lines 88–90).

4.6 Discuss why opinions and beliefs may be considered to be two different things and write down an explanation.

4.7 Marsden uses phrases like 'this stuff' and 'plug it'. Why do you think he does so?

4.8 Discuss the language and the organisation of this excerpt. Why do you think Marsden begins as he does? Is the organisation of the material logical? Is it persuasive? Is the language he uses appropriate for his purpose?

4.9 Writing
Write a contribution to Marsden's book *This I Believe*.

5 EVALUATION

Peter Porter
'A Consumer's Report'

poem

Finally, after many experiences you can evaluate the life you have chosen to live; after all, you are the 'consumer'.

BETWEEN THE LINES

Read the poem on pages 148 and 149 and then complete the following questions and activities.

5.1 What is a 'consumer's report'?

5.2 Explain the metaphor used by the poet. How is the metaphor maintained (or 'extended') throughout the poem?

5.2 A definition of 'metaphor' appears in the Key Terms section of the Appendix.

5.5 A definition of 'irony' appears in the Key Terms section of the Appendix.

5.6 You could also refer to activity 3.1 in Chapter 3 (page 61) and activity 8.2 in Chapter 4 (page 100) for models.

5.3 List the criticisms that the consumer makes about the 'Life' product?

5.4 List the positive comments the poet makes about Life.

5.5 The poet's main technique, apart from the metaphor, is irony. Explain the irony in, for example, 'the price is much too high' (line 22), ' it doesn't keep / yet it's very difficult to get rid of' (lines 33 and 34) and the final three lines.

5.6 Write a comment on the poem, based on the previous activities. You should write about 300 to 400 words.

5.7 Writing
Try your hand at writing a description using an extended metaphor.

> The name of the product I tested is *Life*,
> I have completed the form you sent me
> and understand that my answers are confidential.
>
> I had it as a gift,
> 5 I didn't feel much while using it,
> in fact I think I'd have liked to be more excited.
> It seemed gentle on the hands
> but left an embarrassing deposit behind.
> It was not economical
> 10 and I have used much more than I thought
> (I suppose I have about half left
> but it's difficult to tell)—
> although the instructions are fairly large
> there are so many of them
> 15 I don't know which to follow, especially
> as they seem to contradict each other,
> I'm not sure such a thing
> should be put in the way of children—
> It's difficult to think of a purpose
> 20 for it. One of my friends says
> it's just to keep its maker in a job.
> Also the price is much too high.
> Things are piling up so fast,
> after all, the world got by
> 25 for a thousand million years
> without this, do we need it now?
> (Incidentally, please ask your man
> to stop calling me 'the respondent',
> I don't like the sound of it.)
> 30 There seems to be a lot of different labels,
> sizes and colours should be uniform,
> the shape is awkward, it's waterproof
> but not heat resistant, it doesn't keep
> yet it's very difficult to get rid of:
> 35 whenever they make it cheaper they seem

    to put less in—if you say you don't
    want it, then it's delivered anyway.
    I'd agree it's a popular product,
    it's got into the language; people
40 even say they're on the side of it.
    Personally I think it's overdone,
    a small thing people are ready
    to behave badly about. I think
    we should take it for granted. If its
45 experts are called philosophers or market
    researchers or historians, we shouldn't
    care. We are the consumers and the last
    law makers. So finally, I'd buy it.
    But the question of a 'best buy'
50 I'd like to leave until I get
    the competitive product you said you'd send.

R and J Johnson (eds), *Second Thoughts*

listening

6 across the DESERT

autobiography

Robyn Davidson
Tracks

Some choices may seem bizarre or even downright dangerous.

BETWEEN THE LINES

Tracks is Robyn Davidson's account of her camel trek across the Australian desert from Alice Springs to the west coast.

The teacher will read the excerpt beginning at the start of Chapter 1 (page 19) with 'I arrived in the Alice at 5 a.m.' and ending on page 20 with 'where men are men and women are an afterthought.' The teacher then reads the excerpt starting on page 24 with 'The next day I got a job in the pub' and ending on page 25 with 'This was going to be harder than I thought, but then it was only the first day.'

Your teacher will read the excerpts.

See the Appendix for guidelines on listening tasks before attempting these questions and activities.

6.1 Robyn appears to be:
   a a very careful planner
   b impulsive but brave
   c extremely confident
   d extremely foolhardy.

6.2 Explain Robyn's 'lunatic idea' in your own words.

6.3 Feral camels are camels:
   a from Afghanistan and India
   b imported to Australia in the 1850s
   c running wild in the desert
   d living on cattle properties.

6.4 What impression does Robyn give of the environment?

6.5 Her comment that the centre of Australia is a place 'where men are men and women are an afterthought' suggests that:
   a women arrived after men
   b women have no value
   c males and females are not equal
   d only really tough men survive.

6.6 The phrase closest in meaning to the word 'exuded' in this context is:
   a conveyed the image
   b sent out like sweat
   c made naked or bare
   d delineated.

6.7 How do you know that Robyn is still determined on her plan after talking to Sallay Mahomet?

6.8 'The style of Robyn Davidson's writing could be described as personal, conversational and detailed.' Write about eight to ten lines giving evidence that supports this statement.

APPENDIX

key to texts and terms

ARGUMENTS

The construction of an argument requires:
- a clear statement of your point of view
- the reasons for your point of view
- evidence to support your reasons
- a strongly stated conclusion.

Your argument should be clearly structured, with an introduction, a body of detail and a conclusion. Take care to make logical links between your points. Linking words such as 'therefore', 'because' and 'if' are common in argument texts.

DRAMA SCRIPTS

Drama scripts are presented in a particular way. The features of the presentation include the following.
- A list of characters is given. Sometimes their positions (such as 'King') or relationships (such as 'GISELDA, daughter of the King; WAYNE, her boyfriend') are specified.
- The act and scene are indicated.
- A description of the stage setting is given.
- Stage directions are given. For example, 'the King, Giselda and their attendants enter from the garden.' Often these appear in brackets.
- The speakers' names are clearly indicated in turn. For example:

   King: No! Giselda, you may NOT have the car tonight!
   Giselda: But Dad, Wayne can't borrow the ute because his dad has to work and that means we can't go out …'
   King: Well! Your options are simple. Stay in or stay in!

- Inverted commas are not used.

You can see another example of drama script presentation on pages 53–4.

A drama script should tell a good story and include an interesting situation and plenty of conflict. The visual impact on the audience is an important consideration. When you are writing a drama script, try to imagine what it may look like on the stage. Your stage directions may have to indicate when and where the actors should move.

Creating a drama script from a prose passage

There is more involved in creating a drama script from a prose passage than simply translating the characters' actions and words into the form described above.

In prose, a good deal of action is described and sometimes conversation is indirectly reported rather than directly reported. For example, in activity 6.3, page 68 you are asked to write a drama script based on a passage that has very little direct speech. For a start, you will need to work out the conversation about the toothache.

You also need to decide how much background (such as the pimple-faced lad's attendance at every Salvation Army rally) should be translated into conversation in the present.

Prose descriptions can change the scene frequently and easily, but this may be harder on stage. In this piece there are many settings: the house, mushrooming in the paddock, going to school, the schoolyard, going home from school and the paddock again. You need to decide how to incorporate the scene changes or how you can manage with fewer scene changes.

EDITORIALS

An editorial is usually written by the editor or senior journalist of a newspaper. Its purpose is to provide a comment on a particular issue in the news—not to report the news. Many editorials are designed to be controversial and spark debate and public comment.

The features of an editorial may include:
- a prominent headline
- bold type
- a summary of the issue
- a clear statement of the writer's opinion
- reasons to support the opinion
- suggestions for future action
- an impersonal, passive voice, shown in phrases such as 'There has been discussion ...' or 'Opinions are divided ...'.
- an assertive, usually serious, tone.

EXPLANATIONS

Explanation texts should have:
- a clear title
- a general introduction and explanation of the topic
- clear and logical stages in the explanation
- a summary.

The features of language used in explanation texts are:
- the use of present tense
- words that show cause and effect, such as 'if', 'because' and 'therefore'
- the use of vocabulary that is appropriate to the readers' age and the topic, such as technical or scientific
- an objective or non-personal 'voice' of the speaker.

FEATURE ARTICLES

A newspaper or magazine feature article differs from a newspaper report in that it is usually longer and more reflective, and includes the opinion of the writer on a topical issue, person or event. The journalist will have studied the subject at some length and will present more detail than might generally be included in a newspaper report.

A feature article may include:
- a clever or eye-catching headline
- an introductory paragraph to attract attention and indicate the main idea
- a line of argument or a storyline
- paragraphs that build on the main idea and add examples and detail
- imaginative language and emotive words to convey opinion
- illustrations, such as photographs, drawings and graphs.

GRAPHS—BAR

An example appears below.

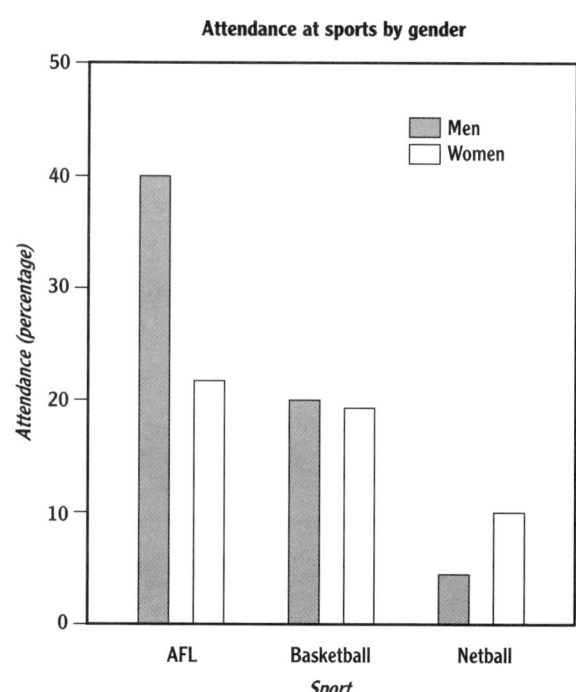

GRAPHS—PIE (OR CIRCLE)

A pie (or circle) graph divides a circle into sectors (slices of pie) to compare amounts. The size of the slices must be in correct proportion. For example, in a pie graph representing students' favourite sports, if 25 per cent of students prefer basketball then one-quarter of the circle must be allocated to basketball. Pie graphs must be carefully labelled because similar sized slices may be difficult to distinguish visually. Colours or shading may be used to improve clarity.

INTERVIEWS

Interviews are spoken 'texts' and you are usually involved in them because you are applying for a job, you are being asked for information because you are an eyewitness to an event or you have expertise in a particular area. An example of a written interview appears on page 39.

The following guidelines apply to job interviews in particular.
- Plan carefully—find out all you can about the organisation that you wish to work for so you can show your knowledge and ask relevant questions at the interview.
- Dress appropriately and be punctual.
- Before and during the interview think carefully about the answers to the questions, so that the type of language you use is appropriate. It's easy to be too casual or even use slang.

The questions you could be asked include the following:
- What qualifications do you have for the position?
- What work experience have you had before? What did you learn from it?
- Why do you want this particular job?
- What are your ambitions for the future?
- What personal qualities do you have that are important to us?
- What are your past achievements at school, in sport or other situations?
- Why is this organisation important to you?
- Would you be willing to study part-time while you work?
- Would you be willing to work overtime?
- What sort of people do you like to work with?

The questions you could ask include:
- Where will I work?
- Who will be my immediate supervisor?
- What does the job involve?
- Will I be able to vary the sorts of tasks I do?
- What opportunities will I have for promotion?
- How will my performance be assessed? by whom?

You may also wish to ask questions regarding wages, transport and uniform if they have not been dealt with previously.

JOB APPLICATIONS

Job applications usually consist of a covering letter and a résumé. The letter should be formal in layout and style, and preferably typed. A sample covering letter and résumé appear on pages 154 and 155.

KEY TERMS

Adjectives
Adjectives are words that are used to describe the qualities of something. Examples include '*tender* passion' and '*sincere* attachment'.

Alliteration
Alliteration is the repetition of a sound (particularly that of a consonant) in words that are close together. It is used to create a particular sound effect. In advertisements it is often used to make the message easier to remember.

Clichés
A cliché is an over-used phrase. An example is 'it's a small world.'

Colloquial language
Colloquial language is language that is more appropriate to everyday speech than to the formality of writing. Colloquial words and phrases are known as 'colloquialisms'. They often include expressions associated with a particular group of people.

Euphemisms
A euphemism is a pleasant sounding or indirect expression that is used to replace an unpleasant or blunt one.

Figures of speech
A figure of speech refers to the non-literal meaning of words. It is used to create an image or for a special effect. An example is 'she hit the nail on the head.' A figure of speech can be termed 'figurative language' and includes metaphor, personification and simile.

Imagery
Imagery is the creation of a 'picture' in words to make the meaning clearer or more interesting or colourful. In the novel excerpt on page 113

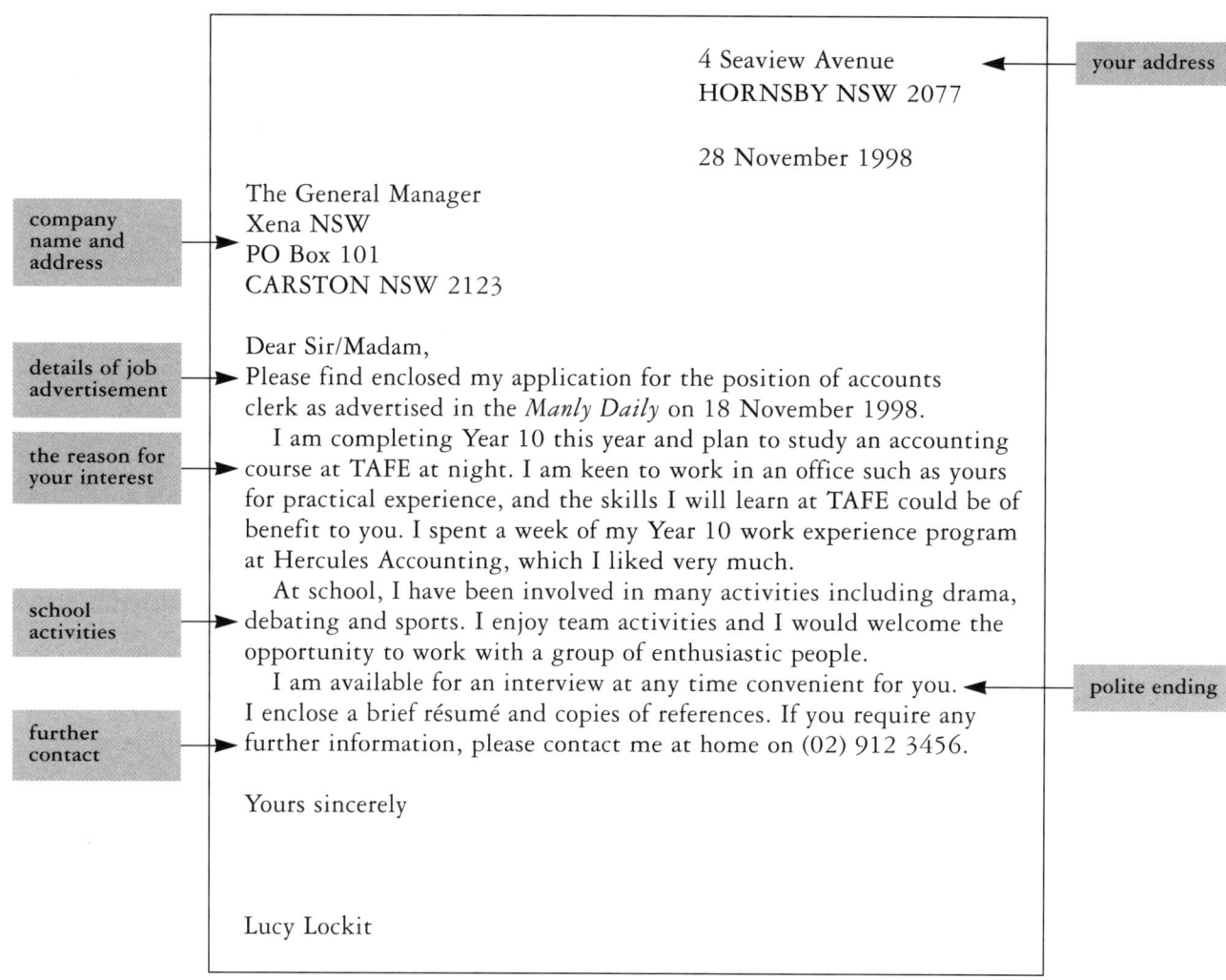

(paragraph 6), the image is of a general who has won a battle at the expense of many dead soldiers.

Imperative verbs
Imperative verbs are words that direct you to *do* something. Examples include *tidy* your room and *clear* your desk!

Irony
There are several types of irony, but irony always involves a difference between what is said and what is intended. The intended meaning may be different from, the opposite of, or an understatement of the surface, or literal, meaning of the words.

Jargon
Jargon is language that belongs to a particular activity or workplace. It can be quite formal but not necessarily understood by everyone. Examples include 'boot', 'wysiwyg' and other words used by computer programmers and operators.

Metaphors
A metaphor is a comparison of two different things for effect. It is stated or suggested that one thing *is* the other to emphasise the similarities even though they may be quite unlike each other. The effect is to create a visual image for the reader. For example, someone may say 'the city is a jungle' or refer to 'the urban jungle'.

A metaphor is said to be 'extended' when the writer continues to build on the comparison throughout a piece of writing. Do not confuse metaphors and similes. Refer to the definition of similes in this section.

Narrative—first person
A story is in the 'first person' when it is told (or narrated) from the point of view of the person telling the story. The pronouns 'I' and 'we' are used. The point of view is restricted to the storyteller's impressions of events and characters.

Résumé

Name:	Lucy Lockit
Address:	4 Seaview Avenue Hornsby NSW 2077
Telephone:	(02) 912 3456
Date of Birth:	29 October 1982
Career Objective:	Accountancy. Enrolled in TAFE Accounting Course, Certificate IV for Account Clerks
Work Experience:	Hercules Accounting Hera Street, Sydney September 1998
Education:	Seaview High School, Hornsby. Years 7–10
Subjects:	English—A, Maths—A, Commerce—A, Computing—A, Geography—A, Japanese—B, History—B
Skills:	Computer—XYZ system Typing—30 words a minute Leadership—captain of school hockey team, 1998
Interests:	Sport (hockey and tennis), reading, travelling and music
References:	Mrs R Bowman Principal Seaview High School Hornsby NSW 2077 Ph.: (02) 912 3455 Mr P Detman Hercules Accounting Hera Street Sydney NSW 2000 Ph.: (02) 912 3454

Narrative—second person
A story is in the second person when the storyteller is directly addressing the reader. The pronoun 'you' is used. Stories in the second person are rare, but advertisements are often written in the second person to create a personal tone.

Narrative—third person
A story is in the 'third person' when it is told or narrated by someone speaking *about* the other characters. The pronouns 'he', 'she', 'it' and 'they' are used. The narrator can switch point of view between the characters. A third-person narrator is sometimes referred to as an 'omniscient' narrator because he or she knows everything about the characters.

Paradox
A paradox is the use of a statement that seems contradictory and therefore absurd, but which actually contains a truth.

Personification
Personification is when objects are given living characteristics to create a stronger image.

Puns
A pun is a play on words to create humour or emphasis. At least two distinct meanings are suggested by the same word or by two similar sounding words, for example '"Right," said the teacher. They picked up their pens.'

Rhetorical questions

Rhetorical questions are ones that do not have to be answered by the reader or the audience, because the answer is implied or answered by the writer or speaker. They are used to make a point effectively, not to request information. This technique attracts the attention of the reader or audience and involves them in the topic. It is often used in speeches.

Satire

Satire is the mocking or ridiculing of human foolishness in a scornful or amusing way. It always involves irony.

Similes

A simile is a comparison where one thing is said to be like another. The words 'like' or 'as' are used in a simile. The ideas or objects being compared may be quite different from each other. However, the simile creates a clear image, for example 'the city is like a jungle.'

When analysing a simile or a metaphor, identify the two things being compared but try to explain why the comparison is suitable and therefore effective.

Slang

Slang is language that is in common use but is considered inappropriate for standard Australian usage in some situations, such as in formal letters. 'Ripper', 'bonzer', 'wicked' and 'filthy' are all slang words. The use of slang can show membership of a particular group.

Tone

The tone of a piece of writing refers to the way the writer *sounds* to the reader. The writer may sound good humoured, angry or sarcastic, or relaxed and casual as in a chatty letter to a good friend. When deciding how to describe tone, consider the message and the word choice.

LETTERS—FORMAL

Formal letters are useful in many situations. You can use them to request or convey information, express a point of view, make a complaint or apply for a job.

An example of a formal letter of application is included in the Job Applications section of this Appendix.

A letter of complaint appears on page 157.

LETTERS—PERSONAL

The structure and layout of a personal letter may be similar to those of a formal letter, but the style may be very different. Personal letters often contain non-standard grammar and may sound like 'written-down speech', with exclamation marks, dashes and incomplete sentences. They may contain colloquialisms and vocabulary that reflect the relationship between the writer and receiver. The tone is likely to be conversational, friendly and warm. The writer will probably use the personal pronoun 'I'.

Examples of personal letters appear on pages 108 and 140–1.

LISTENING TASKS

Listening tasks should be based on about five or six minutes of material. Suitable material includes a reading from a story or play, a radio program, a speech, a conversation or a class presentation.

The questions need to test knowledge of:
- the content or main ideas
- the vocabulary
- the purpose of the material
- the intended audience
- the attitudes of the speaker(s) and/or writer(s).

Use the following guidelines:
- multiple-choice, true or false and short-answer questions should be used
- the students should have a copy of the questions, and paper on which to write the answers
- the listening material could be read out or taped and played to the class
- the students should read through the questions before they listen to the material
- the students should make notes while they listen to the material
- play or read the material to the class, read the questions to the class and then play or read the material again
- allow about ten minutes for the students to write the answers to the questions.

The class, working in groups could also devise listening activities. They could prepare a reading from a novel, short story, poem, play or an article from the media. They could write their own script and present it to the class.

Type up the questions and give a copy to each student, use an overhead projector or write the

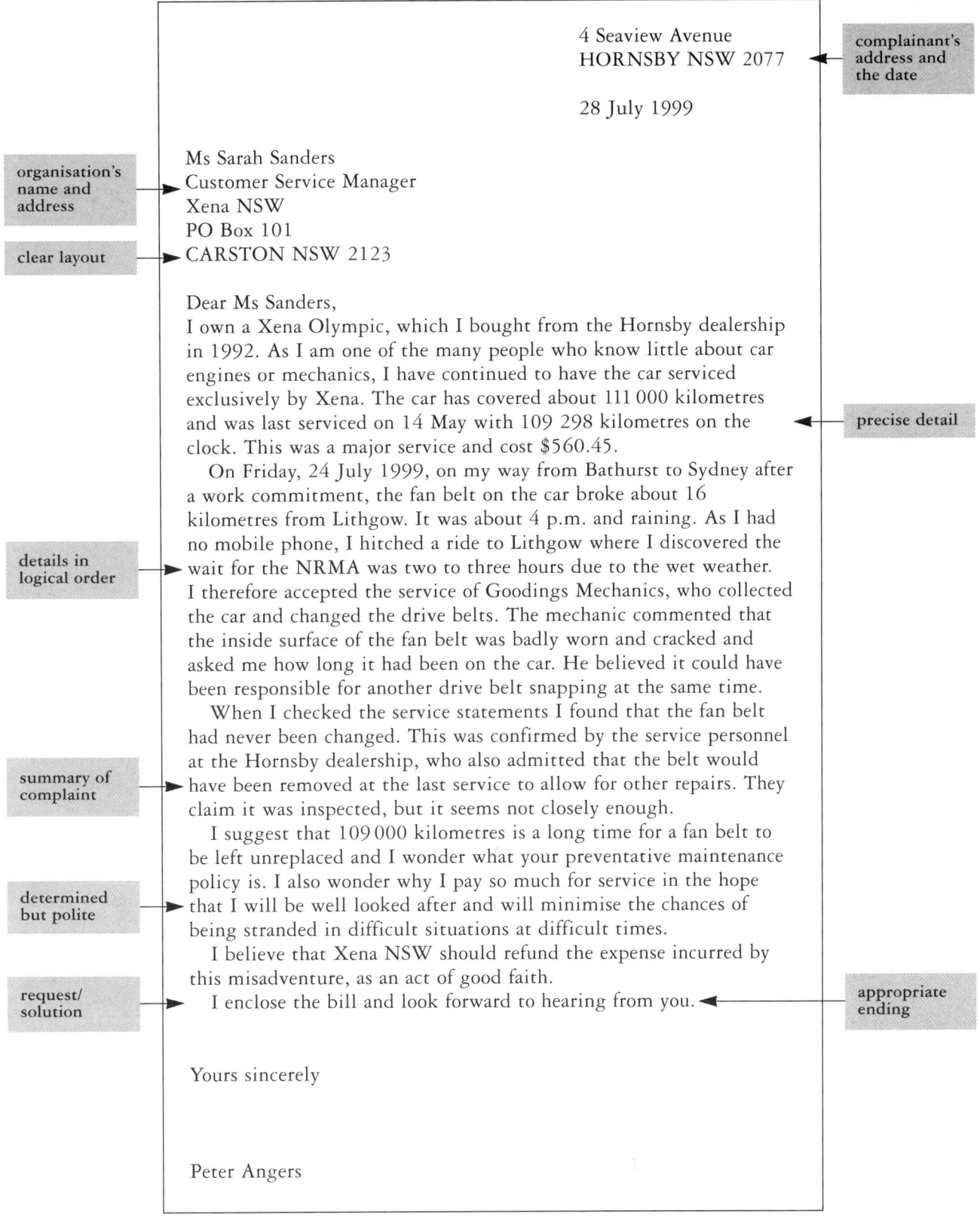

APPENDIX 157

questions clearly on the board. The answers could be peer assessed.

MULTIPLE-CHOICE QUESTIONS

Multiple-choice questions should have a stem and four possible answers (usually referred to as distractors) to choose from. Each distractor should correctly complete the sentence that begins with the stem. The distractor should only contain one idea. One distractor should be the correct answer. The other three distractors should be answers that are close to correct or are obviously wrong but not nonsensical.

The following question is from Chapter 1 (p. 5).

1.6 'Let's stereotype' (paragraph 9) suggests that the writer is going to:
   a listen to what the tribes say
   b make a mould
   c describe people
   d put people in categories.

To answer this question you will need to find the meaning of 'stereotype' in your dictionary. Then consider its meaning *in its context*, that is the meaning depends on the ideas being expressed in the text. To stereotype does mean to make a mould (it comes from the process of typesetting), but the writer here does not mean that she is going to make a mould. However, the word clearly means more than just listening to or describing people. Therefore d is the best answer in context. The writer intends to put people into groups or categories according to their looks and behaviour (which are a type of mould or pattern).

The following question is from Chapter 3 (p. 55).

1.8 'With feigning voice, verses of feigning love' (line 12) suggests that:
   a Lysander's songs are faint
   b Lysander has written and sung songs to impress Hermia
   c Lysander's poetry is not his own
   d Lysander's love is not genuine.

Once again you will need to check your dictionary for the meanings of the words used in the question and possible answers. In this question, option a is obviously wrong because 'faint' has nothing to do with the word 'feigning'. While the statement in option b is true—Lysander does appear to have done these things—the speaker, Egeus, is saying not just that Lysander has done them, but that they were deceptive actions. Note the meaning of 'feigning'. Option c is not quite correct because Lysander sang in addition to composing poetry. Is option d therefore the better answer because the meaning echoes the sense of the original?

NARRATIVE STRUCTURE

Narratives begin with an introduction (or orientation) to people, places, events and ideas. This often includes, or suggests, one or more complications, such as an unexpected event, a change or a conflict.

The central character or characters must take action to respond to the complication. This action results in a series of events that develop the plot, the characterisation and the themes. These often become more complex, exciting or dangerous and lead to a crisis or climax. This is the most exciting, frightening or poignant part of the story. Often it is also a turning point that leads to the resolution.

The resolution is a conclusion of the complication and is sometimes referred to as the denouement. It usually represents a development of understanding of the central character(s). Denouement is a French word for 'unknotting', so it suggests an unravelling of complications or mysteries.

NEWSPAPER REPORTS

The purpose of a newspaper report is to present factual, impersonal reports of current events. However, opinions are often implied through word choice.

Newspaper reports have the following features.
- An eye-catching headline captures the reader's attention. The words used in the headline and the size at which it is printed are both important. The words used may be emotive and sensational or alliterative, or rely on cliché and pun for effect.
- Opening statements point to the event (what?), the place (where?), the time (when?), those involved (who?) and the reason (why?).
- The body of the report develops the detail with the use of background information and/or discussion of the consequences.
- Detail is developed in a logical way.
- Sentence construction is clear.
- Use is often made of eyewitness accounts or an expert's comment on the situation.
- The present tense is often used, but the past tense may be appropriate in the case of, for example, a traffic accident.
- Both direct and indirect speech are used.
- There are often photos or diagrams. If so, they

are placed for maximum effect to catch the reader's attention.
- Reports traditionally fade into 'filler' details. These are extra, but less important, details and comment that can be deleted by the editor, according to the space available for the story.

SENTENCE STRUCTURE

Sentences vary in length and complexity. Short, simple sentences can make meaning very clear, while longer, more complex ones slow the reader down and may need more thought. When writers use varying sentence lengths, for example a short sentence after a long one, it usually means they want to emphasise something.

A simple sentence usually contains one idea: 'I am watching a movie.' Compound sentences are made up of simple sentences that are joined by 'and', 'but' or 'or': 'I should be studying but I am going to the movies.'

Complex sentences are made up of several clauses or parts but they can be formal in tone, rather than conversational like a loose sentence. The following example is from *Tom Jones* (see p. 113): 'The thoughts of leaving her almost rent his heart asunder, but the consideration of reducing her to ruin and beggary still racked him, if possible, more; and if the violent desire of possessing her person could have induced him to listen one moment to this alternative, still he was by no means certain of her resolution to indulge his wishes at so high an expense.'

A loose sentence contains many ideas, presented one after another, in a conversational flow: 'I'm just watching this movie, Mum, and then I'll do the garbage because I don't want to lose the plot, which is really complicated, and I won't miss the garbage truck so don't worry.'

SETTING

The setting of a piece of writing refers to the physical setting (where), the time (when) and sometimes the atmosphere (such as cold and frightening, or warm and happy).

SPEECHES

A speech is a personal address to an audience. Speeches can be used for a variety of purposes. For example, a speech may present an argument (as in a debate or a political speech), present information or provide an entertaining and/or amusing experience for the audience, as in an after-dinner speech.

The purpose of the speech is the key to its organisation. If it is presenting an argument, then it needs to refer to the features of argument and so on.

The features of a speech may include:
- an introduction that attracts the audience's attention
- the use of personal, funny stories and anecdotes
- quotations
- controversial statements and rhetorical questions
- language that is appropriate for the audience
- the use of a few simply expressed, important points
- interesting examples
- a well-paced (not too fast) delivery
- brevity.

STYLE

Style in written or spoken texts refers to the particular way a writer or speaker arranges words to achieve his or her purpose.

When you are discussing the style of a writer or speaker, it may be useful to pretend that you are explaining the purpose and function of the Sydney Opera House to a visitor from another planet. You would need to explain its purpose, its highly unusual shape and the materials with which it is built. Then you would take your intergalactic visitor inside and discuss the internal finish and the beautiful views from inside the building and what effect these have on most people.

In the same way, when you read a piece of writing or listen to a speech, you need to identify its purpose. The purpose, and the period in which it is written or spoken, will have a good deal to do with its shape. A report on the front page of a daily newspaper looks quite different from a feature article in a magazine. Paragraph and sentence length and structure may vary. A detailed, descriptive passage from a novel will be quite different in purpose and shape from a casual conversation in a modern drama script.

The building materials of style include:
- the level of language, such as formal, informal/conversational, colloquial or slang
- the use of first-, second- or third-person narrative
- paragraph structure, that is the organisation of ideas
- sentence length and structure, such as simple, complex or balanced

- word choice, such as emotive, objective or technical
- imagery, such as metaphor, personification, simile or symbolism
- sound devices, such as rhythm, repetition, rhyme, alliteration or assonance.

Finally, you need to consider the effect that the speech or piece of writing has on the audience or reader. Does it convey information, ideas, emotions or atmosphere well?

SUMMARIES

To summarise written material is to reduce it to the most important points. You should arrange the points in a logical order.

VISUAL TEXTS— ANALYSIS

Visual texts, such as photographs, drawings and advertisements, need to be studied and analysed as carefully as written or spoken texts. Visual texts have their own 'language' and you need to be able to analyse the composition (how the image is 'made up' or comprised) of a visual text through this language.

The questions to ask when you are studying a visual text are as follows.

- What is being pictured? what is the subject?
- How are the parts of the picture arranged? what is centred? what is in the foreground? what is in the background? is some part of the subject placed off centre?
- What relationships are suggested between the parts?
- What colours, or shades of black and white, are used for various parts of the picture?
- Is there eye contact between the subject(s) and the viewer? Does it suggest honesty? defiance? an offer? a request? a demand? or something else?
- From what angle is the image pictured? from above? from below? at the same level? What effect does this have?
- How close is the viewer to the picture? What difference does this make?
- Does the picture suggest action? or is it a static, or still, view of the subject?
- Does the viewer's eye tend to move across the picture or up and down the picture? For example, if the eye tends to move up, there could be a suggestion that something at the top of the picture is important or that we are being asked to 'look up to' something. Similarly, if the eye moves from left to right, does this convey a particular message?
- Are there any particular images or symbols in the picture? signs? words? an Australian flag? a lifesaver's cap? green and gold? particular shapes? repetition of a particular object or colour?

Answering these questions should help you to make some judgments about the composition of a visual text.